Creative Encounters with Creative People

Written by Janice Gudeman
Portraits by Mark Beebe
Illustrations by Vanessa Filkins

Cover by Kathryn Hyndman
Copyright © Good Apple, Inc., 1984
ISBN No. 0-86653-258-7
Printing No. 87654321

GOOD APPLE, INC.
BOX 299
CARTHAGE, IL 62321-0299

FOREWORD

Here is a book that will challenge not only children but adults! No doubt the most motivating experience in life is to read about other people—particularly those who have overcome difficult circumstances both within themselves and within their environments and yet emerge as creative people who make unusual contributions to others and the societies in which they live.

One time when I was disillusioned and in emotional turmoil, I studied the lives of people who were used in special ways. As I read, I noticed a pattern. I saw that suffering was often used to eventually enable them to help others who were going through the same deep waters. That sudden insight changed my psychological disposition. It enabled me to experience joy in the midst of turmoil and to make sense out of what seemed chaotic.

I'm reminded of the first time I became acquainted with Helen Keller and her story. It was life changing! I'll never forget the impact on my life.

Janice Gudeman brings you into this great woman's life and lets you touch "the hem of her garment." You, too, will be challenged—and different—because of this encounter.

And there are many more people you'll get to know who will spark your own creative talents—as a teacher, a student, a parent or a child. I recommend it greatly.

Gene A. Getz, Ph.D.

ii

ACKNOWLEDGMENTS

I want to express my deep appreciation to my family, my 94-year-old grandfather, relatives, and friends. I thank them for their love and inspiration and for saying, "You can do it!" With admiration and respect I thank them for being examples to me. Their influence on my life has been profound. Their lives are reflected in this book.

I am thankful to my cousin Gene Getz for writing the foreword. Dr. Gene and Elaine Getz gave me special encouragement in writing this book.

I extend my appreciation to Marian Anderson, Mary Kay Ash, Sam Butcher, Dr. James Dobson, Dr. Gene Getz, Peter Jenkins, Joni Eareckson Tada, Maria von Trapp, and Zig Ziglar for their support in being a part of this book. Their lives are an inspiration to me. My hope is that their lives as portrayed in this book will influence many people.

I would like to express sincere gratitude to Joni Eareckson Tada and Sam Butcher for sharing their artwork in this book. Judy Crane, the assistant to Sam Butcher, was a special help in developing his section.

I wish to thank the creative people of Good Apple: Gary Grimm, Sharon Thompson, and Barbara Ancelet. I appreciate their cooperation, hard work, ideas and expertise.

I am grateful to my cousin Dan Getz and to my friend Nancy Berry for their poems.

I thank my students who were involved in field testing this book. Their creativity, enthusiasm, and childlike love for life greatly inspired me while I was writing this book. They are special, and I encourage them to use their potential.

DEDICATION

This book is affectionately dedicated to my family: Dad and Mom, my brother Darrel, and my sister Bev and her family. Their inspiration, wisdom, guidance, encouragement, and love have enriched my life immeasurably. Thank you for being you.

TABLE OF CONTENTS

Souls That Touch

I am everyone I have ever met;
There are no chance acquaintances.
Those that were kind
Taught me empathy.
Those who were patient
Let me see that
Being first was not important.
Those that loved me
Even in my frailties
Showed me an enormous gift
That would carry me
Through difficult times.
Those that were intolerant of me
Proved that someday
Others would fill this void.
And those who stood
For deep hatred
Portrayed a side of life
I was glad not to be
A member of.
I am everyone
I have ever met.
What am I teaching you?

Nancy Berry

HOW TO USE THIS BOOK

Travel through the journey of life and capture the opportunity to meet creative people who will inspire and challenge you. Touch the lives of Helen Keller, George Washington Carver, Jim Thorpe, and nineteen other exemplary people of the past and present. Identify with their characteristics and their successes and failures to help spark your own creative talents, overcome hardships, and build and fulfill your own goals in life.

Each unit includes quotations, a Biographical Sketch, Creative Encounters, Independent Projects, and Resource Books.

The quotations and poems in this book can be analyzed and used as topics for inspirational discussions and/or creative writing.

A Biographical Sketch provides factual information to introduce the life of each person.

The Creative Encounters offer opportunities of enrichment for open-ended discussions, brainstorming, researching, creative problem solving, creative writing, creative drama, and hands-on experiences. The Creative Encounters are a variety of activities designed to be used with a group of students in a teacher-directed setting. However, many of the activities could be adapted for a student working alone. The written and oral expression of the activities can be varied and adapted to fit the needs and interests of your group. The learning atmosphere should reflect warmth, care, empathy, encouragement, and enthusiasm for learning.

Independent Projects provide ideas for independent study to enhance higher levels of thinking. Independent study helps students to develop self-motivation, self-confidence, and various skills, which will help them to continue learning throughout their lives. Students work individually or in small groups. They select a topic, develop the questions, set goals, gather resources, research, develop a product, share the project, and evaluate the independent study. The goals of the teacher are to act as a resource person, provide guidance and enthusiasm for learning, and encourage quality work. The contract for the independent projects is included as a format to plan the projects. (See page x.)

The Resource Books provide a variety of references for the activities in Creative Encounters and Independent Projects to aid in the study of each person.

A certificate of excellence is designed to praise and reward students for their outstanding achievements and successes as they journey into the pages of *Creative Encounters with Creative People*.

HOW CAN PARENTS HELP DEVELOP THEIR CHILD'S POTENTIAL?

Dear Parents,
This book provides the opportunity for you to discover the joy of learning with your child. With admiration and respect your child looks to you as an example.

- Accept your child with love and understanding. Essentially, your child has the same needs as other children. Your child has the need to hear the reassuring words "I love you."
- Work with your child on an older intellectual level. Recognize your child's intellectual maturity. Expect him to understand as an older child would.
- Remember he is a child, not a little adult, and he needs to live the life of a child. Care must be taken not to overemphasize his abilities in front of others.
- Help your child learn from life while he is young. Encourage your child's natural history.
- Challenge your child to try his solutions, to learn to test his ideas. Parents make a great contribution by encouraging a child to think situations through and consider the consequences. Be available. However, sometimes it is wise to wait until he asks for help.
- Read to your child. Encourage your child to read.
- Provide a variety of learning materials. Present activities such as the following:

  1. Discover new uses for materials such as automobile tires or umbrellas.
  2. Make up a code and write messages.
  3. Estimate distances, and pace off the distance to check the answers.

- Provide enriching experiences, such as music lessons.
- Provide a relaxed home relationship that is conducive to discussion and counsel. Your child needs you to listen to him.
- Be sensitive to your child's needs, and do everything possible to meet his needs.
- Praise your child, and inspire him to use his potential.
- Use these important phrases: "That's a great idea." "Tell me more about what you want to know." "That's a good question. Let's find out." "What do you think about that?" "Try it. Go ahead. I'll help you when you need it."
- Encourage friendships.
- Visit libraries, museums, planetariums, zoos, nature spots, concerts, and other places.
- Read and discuss various resource materials and research that provide helpful suggestions and other information, such as characteristics of gifted children.
- Discover opportunities to use his talents now and in preparation for future goals and career plans.
- Demonstrate respect for education. Discover the joy of learning together.

BOUNDARY BREAKERS

Boundary breakers are questions throughout this book in the Creative Encounters. This technique helps to build confidence in the ability to discuss and relate to others. Boundary breakers are designed to develop speaking and listening skills while students learn more about themselves and others.

Boundary breakers can be used to introduce a lesson, to spark interest in an upcoming topic, or to rebuild unity at the end of a lesson. These questions provoke a higher level of thought and make learning relevant and personal to the students. Listening and acceptance are essential to the success of boundary breaking.

Instructions: Leader

1. Sit in a circle.
2. The leader states the question and calls upon a student within the circle. This person responds; the person to the right or left responds next.
3. The leader is a participant and responds to the question, also.
4. The leader is a model of keen interest and listening.
5. The leader should vary the questions, beginning with a light one and proceeding to deep, thought-provoking ones.

Instructions: Participants

1. Each person is to answer according to the way that he interprets the questions. There will be no discussion or debate.
2. When a person needs more time to ponder and reflect, this can be indicated by saying "pass." The leader returns to this person at the end of the first round of questions for a response. At this time if the person wishes not to respond, this can be indicated by "pass-pass." Passes are to be accepted with as much positive acceptance as any response.
3. While each person is answering, observe and learn more about others.
4. The key word is "listen."

Examples of Boundary Breakers

1. If you could have dinner with any famous person, whom would you choose?
2. If you could learn a new sport, what sport would you like to learn?
3. What is your favorite time of day?
4. What color do you think of when you think of happiness?
5. How would you describe yourself to someone who does not know you?
6. If you could interview George Washington, what would you discuss?
7. If you were making a record about nature and animals, what sounds would you add?
8. If someone wrote a book about you, what would you like the title to be?
9. Share some things for which you are thankful.
10. What do you think is the world's most serious problem?
11. If you became a leader in the United States government, what steps would you take to help our country?
12. What are some ways to show respect for people?

ENCOUNTER LESSONS

Encounter lessons are in the Creative Encounters of Wolfgang Amadeus Mozart, Henry Ford, and George Washington Carver. Encounter lessons are activities to stimulate creativity and positive feelings of worth. These enrichment lessons provide an "encounter" with ideas and others. The goals of the leader are to help the students feel valuable and to see learning as relevant to their individual needs. The learning atmosphere should reflect acceptance and understanding, for this provides each student an opportunity to bring his uniqueness to the task.

1. These active lessons are usually in small groups of eight to ten and last approximately twenty minutes. They work well with any age.
2. The student is asked to become something else and respond as though he is this new thing. The student might become a ski, a rose, an eagle, or a page in a book.
3. Each time a question is asked, the leader starts with a different participant, and each student responds in turn.
4. After the lesson, the leader talks with the participants about how they viewed their encounter and asks how they felt about being something else. The discussion then turns to the audience, and they give their reactions to the encounter group.
5. The encounter lesson should then be followed by extenders, which are a wide variety of activities that would be related to the lesson. The encounter lesson has served to promote interest in the area to be studied and to develop the higher levels of thinking.

The instructions for the boundary breakers and encounter lessons are adapted from Dr. Dorothy Sisk of the University of South Florida in Tampa.

BRAINSTORMING

Brainstorming is a technique in Creative Encounters and in Independent Projects. Brainstorming is a process of free, creative thinking used by a group of people to generate many ideas.

1. Someone records the ideas.
2. Encourage everyone to contribute ideas.
3. No criticism, discussion, or evaluation is allowed until the idea generation is completed.
4. Quantity of ideas is a goal.
5. Funny or imaginative ideas are acceptable.
6. Build on others' ideas and work with others in the combination of ideas.
7. After the brainstorming is completed, each idea is evaluated. Ideas are selected, combined, and organized into solutions.

MY INDEPENDENT PROJECT

Title: _____

A brief explanation of my project: _____
_____

Some questions I want to answer: _____
_____
_____

Materials needed: _____
_____
_____

Resources (books, encyclopedias, people, and others): _____
_____
_____

Ideas for sharing my project: _____
_____
_____

Estimation of time needed to complete my project: _____
_____

Date started: _____

Date completed: _____

Steps I will take:

Step 1 _____

Step 2 _____

Step 3 _____

Step 4 _____

Step 5 _____

_____   _____
Advisor's Signature   Student's Signature

CERTIFICATE OF EXCELLENCE

Creative Encounters with Creative People

This honor is proudly bestowed upon

_____

for demonstrating scholarly, academic and research achievement and superior creative thinking.

Signature _____

Date _____

JOHNNY

As a boy, Johnny remembers a time
When he was led astray by a mere little dime.
The store clerk gave Dad an extra ten cents;
Why he didn't give it back just didn't make sense.

Johnny was watching, unknown to Father;
Dad thought, "Why give it back? It's just a bother."
Johnny learned that day from Father's action
That it's okay to bend the rules, if just by a fraction.

The next time involved Mother and the telephone.
She always said to tell the truth; a lie she never would condone.
But that day was different—Miss Smith was on the phone;
Mom wanted Johnny to tell her she was not at home.

Miss Smith always talked so very long—
Mother didn't think what she'd done was wrong,
But that day Johnny learned that it's okay to lie.
It still seemed wrong, but he didn't know why.

As Johnny got older through the years,
He paid close attention to a few of his peers.
One in particular was Johnny's best friend;
He thought he was one on whom he could depend.

But that day in school they were taking a test,
And Johnny's friend looked on his paper rather than guess.
Johnny was ready to go and tell,
But his friend convinced him that it was best not to fail.

When Johnny got older, he silently watched the people in power,
But his country was in trouble at a critical hour.
He soon found out that even they
Said things that seemed wrong were perfectly okay.

They said it was okay to kill an unborn baby.
The choice was the woman's—to be or not to be.
Johnny felt this was wrong deep down in his heart,
But so many people were taking part!

As Johnny was being executed for murder and robbery,
He asked himself, "Why am I the one who must pay the penalty?
They're the ones who taught me to steal, kill, cheat and lie,
And now I'm the one they say must die!"

The point to be made is easy to see.
What people see in you they may someday be.
So always be careful of what you do,
'Cause a "Johnny" could be watching *you!*

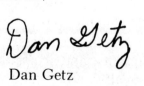

Dan Getz

Dan Getz
Age 17

xii

HANS CHRISTIAN ANDERSEN

"The story of my life to this moment lies unrolled before me, more rich and beautiful than I could have imagined it. I feel that I am a child of fortune; nearly all have met me with kindness and friendship; very seldom has my trust in my fellow men been deceived. From the prince to the poorest peasant I have found noble human hearts.

"Rich and serenely happy, my life is a beautiful fairy tale. I had experienced what it was to be poor and lonely, and to move in luxurious surroundings; I had experienced being scorned and honored. The history of my life will say to the world what it says to me—there is a loving God, who directs all things for the best."

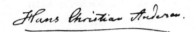

BIOGRAPHICAL SKETCH

Hans was a sensitive child, and he preferred daydreaming, playing with his puppet theater made by his father, reading, and making up stories. His father had hoped to live a scholarly life, but his own parents' farmhouse had burned, and he was required to earn a living as a shoemaker. He often read stories from the classics to Hans; they were outdoor companions, too, roaming the woods around Odense, Denmark. Hans' mother, Ane Marie, a proud, ambitious woman, washed clothes in the river to make a little extra money to help her family earn a living.

To Hans, home meant the place to find all the tenderness, sympathy, and love that a small boy could need. His mother took pride in their one-room home and worked hard to polish and clean. Hans made up stories about everything in the room. In his imagination the polished pots and pans were his friends, and they came alive and talked to him. To Hans, their little home was a world of adventure in which anything might happen.

Hans' father made toys for him, and they spent hours playing with puppets, dressing them, and making up plays for them to act out. Since the other boys did not want to be with him, Hans lived in his dream world. He would have played with the other boys, but they thought he was tall and awkward and had different ideas, so they mocked him and chased him through the streets.

After his father's death, Hans decided he wanted to see the world. His mother wanted him to become an apprentice to an Odense tailor, but his great ambition was to go to Copenhagen at the age of fourteen. He intended to become famous and to fulfill his dreams. He believed that people must first suffer and go through a great deal of trouble, after which they would succeed and become famous.

Hans Christian Andersen traveled throughout Europe. His first fairy tales were published in 1835 in the book *Fairy Tales for Children*. From 1835 until his death in 1875, he published more than thirty books. During his lifetime Odense, his birthplace, where he had been mocked as a child, was acknowledged for his greatness. This much-loved storyteller was admired for his kindness, imagination, simplicity, and his childlike spirit. Hans Christian Andersen, who became a close friend of European royalty and of the distinguished figures of his day, is acclaimed by the world for his contributions to literature.

Most of our time in school is spent memorizing facts and figures and answering questions based on these facts and figures. This is called cognitive and convergent thinking. However, it is also very important to learn to think divergently—that is, to use your imaginations, to create new ideas and discover new things.

Let's have some fun with divergent thinking as we take a zany trip to the zoo. As you answer the following questions, remember that there are no right or wrong answers. So throw caution to the wind and let your imaginations soar!

1. If you crossed a giraffe with a hippopotamus, you'd have a giraffopotamus or a hippopoteraffe! What would you get if you crossed a lion with a monkey? A snake with a zebra? Brainstorm all sorts of other silly combinations of animals found at the zoo.

2. Would you rather be a camel or an elephant? Explain your answer.

3. Choose a wild animal that you'd like to domesticate. What would you use it for?

4. Pretend you are a gorilla living in the jungle and are captured and taken to live at the zoo. Describe your feelings.

CREATIVE ENCOUNTER #2.........Group Discussion

Hans Christian Andersen's story *The Ugly Duckling* is symbolic of Andersen's life. Read *The Ugly Duckling* to the class. Then divide the class into groups and have each group answer and discuss the following questions:

1. Why did the hen, wild ducks, and others make fun of the duckling?
2. Do you feel the cat and hen had the right attitude toward the duckling? Why or why not?
3. Why was the duckling later loved by the children and his friends?
4. What do you think might have happened if the duckling had gone back to visit his barnyard after he had grown to be a swan? What would you do and how would you feel if you were the duckling and were misunderstood by others?
5. What would you do and how would you feel if you were the duckling's brother or sister?
6. How should you react and feel toward others who are different? How would you want others to feel toward you in this situation?
7. Explain the parallel between *The Ugly Duckling* and Andersen's life.
8. Explain the following sayings: "Beauty is only skin deep." "Beauty is in the eye of the beholder." "Pretty is as pretty does." How can the meanings of these sayings be related to *The Ugly Duckling*, to Andersen's life, and to your life?

CREATIVE ENCOUNTER #3.........Thinking Skills

Dr. J. P. Guilford identified five intellectual operations in his theory of the Structure of Intellect. They are the following:

cognitive thinking—recognition, awareness, understanding
memorization—recall
evaluation—judgement or comparison
convergent thinking—pulling facts together in order to find a single answer
divergent thinking—creative, imaginative thinking

Read each of the following sentences and decide if the sentence is an example of cognitive thinking, memorization, evaluation, convergent thinking or divergent thinking. Write your answer in the space to the left of each sentence. (You may decide that some of the sentences require a combination of operations. If so, list all the operations.)

_____ Think of all the ways you could make a teddy bear more fun.

_____ Do you think it's fair to take an animal from the forest and place him in a zoo?

_____ How do you spell the name of the animal that roars?

_____ Name an African animal that is similar to the American deer.

_____ Name one African and one Asian animal that are both black and white.

3

CREATIVE ENCOUNTER #4.........Accomplishing Goals

Although Hans Christian Andersen's mother wanted him to stay in Odense and become a tailor, Hans was determined to pursue his dream of becoming an actor. So Hans left home to go to Copenhagen to sing, dance and act. However, he was so tall, thin and awkward that audiences only laughed at him. Discouraged but unwilling to give up, Hans decided that if he couldn't be an actor, he would try his hand at writing. Although not a scholar, Hans showed great talent at humorous writing and became famous throughout the world for his creative and imaginative stories.

Hans Christian Andersen's life is a true success story and serves as an inspiration to all those who have hopes and dreams for the future.

1. What are your goals for the future? _____

_____

2. Will it be easy or difficult for you to achieve your goals? What kinds of sacrifices, if any, will you need to make? _____

_____

3. Describe a situation in which you or someone you know sacrificed an immediate reward in order to accomplish a long-range goal. _____

_____

4. Below are some personal characteristics which have been found to contribute to achievement and success. Read over all the characteristics and then try to decide which are most important to success and which are least important. Rank these in order from 1—10 with #1 being the most important and #10 the least important.

_____ optimism   _____ perseverance

_____ health   _____ willingness to take risks

_____ patience   _____ peer/family support

_____ self-confidence   _____ money

_____ courage   _____ ability to delay gratification

Can you think of any other qualities important to achieving goals? If so, list those qualities. _____

_____

5. Is there ever a point at which you should redirect your goals? If you fail over and over again, should you continue trying? What does "being realistic" mean to you? Do you think that perhaps Hans' goal of becoming an actor might have been unrealistic? Write your thoughts and feelings about this subject on a separate sheet of paper.

CREATIVE ENCOUNTER #5..........Drawing a Caricature

A caricature is a drawing exaggerating distinctive characteristics of an individual. Drawing a caricature can be a way to learn to laugh at yourself. Your caricature can be an expression of your sense of humor. At first it may be difficult to talk about yourself, but this is a fun way to begin.

Ask yourself these questions to help you think of ideas for your caricature. What is special about you? What is a special or different quality, feature, or characteristic about yourself? What are your interests?

Draw a caricature of yourself and write about it, perhaps in the form of a limerick, on a separate sheet of paper.

Share your caricatures with others. Display them on a bulletin board.

INDEPENDENT PROJECTS—ANDERSEN

1. Make up your own fairy tale and illustrate it. Write guidelines and rules for a "Best Fairy Tale" contest. Select judges and give awards to the winners.
2. Draw caricatures of famous people or your favorite things.
3. Hans Christian Andersen's admiration for royalty and his love for poor and simple people, birds, flowers, and things that are beautiful are reflected in his stories. Study and analyze the meanings and messages of Andersen's fairy tales.
4. Compare how the events in Andersen's fairy tales relate to his real-life experiences. Relate your own experiences in your comparisons.
5. Illustrate and write a creative story from the viewpoint of a flower, a kitten, or a stuffed animal.
6. Hans Christian Andersen had a talent for cutting the most amusing and delicate pictures out of paper—storks in their nests, windmills, and flying balloons. He did this with dexterity and speed. Many of these fragile paper cutouts are still in existence. People thought they were so pretty that they took care to preserve them. Make various designs by cutting and folding paper.
7. Study the techniques to develop your skills in storytelling. Make a chart of these techniques. For example, whatever your characters may be, give them names, voices, and personalities. Breathe life into them, and they will become so real to you that you and your listeners will forget that they are not human.
8. Hans Christian Andersen was very sensitive, and one harsh word or unkind criticism seemed to outweigh many kind and favorable ones. Write a letter of advice to Hans Christian Andersen concerning this problem.

RESOURCE BOOKS—ANDERSEN

Andersen, Hans Christian. *The Fairy Tale of My Life*. New York: Paddington Press Ltd., 1975.

Andersen, Hans Christian. *Hans Christian Andersen's Fairy Tales*. London: Paul Hamlyn, 1959.

Andersen, Hans Christian. *The Ugly Duckling*. New York: Charles Scribner's Sons, 1965.

Andersen, Hans Christian. *The Ugly Duckling, The Princess Who Tended Geese*. New York: McCall Publishing Co., 1969.

Bredsdorff, Elias. *Hans Christian Andersen: The Story of His Life and Work, 1805-75*. New York: Charles Scribner's Sons, 1975.

Collin, Hedvig. *Young Hans Christian Andersen*. New York: The Viking Press, 1955.

Garst, Shannon. *Hans Christian Andersen: Fairy Tale Author*. Boston: Houghton Mifflin Co., 1965.

Godden, Rumer. *Hans Christian Andersen: A Great Life in Brief*. New York: Alfred A. Knopf, 1954.

Manning-Sanders, Ruth. *The Story of Hans Andersen: The Swan of Denmark*. New York: E.P. Dutton & Co., Inc., 1950.

Montgomery, Elizabeth Rider. *Hans Christian Andersen: Immortal Storyteller*. Champaign, Illinois: Garrard Publishing Co., 1968.

Wheeler, Opal. *Hans Andersen: Son of Denmark*. New York: E.P. Dutton & Co., 1951.

Williams, Margery. *The Velveteen Rabbit*. New York: Doubleday & Co., Inc., 1958.

MARIAN ANDERSON

"Singing was a serious business with me, and I had a deep sense of responsibility about my work with the choirs. Singing in the presence of other people seemed to me a normal activity all through the years of growing up. I loved to sing. My heart was filled when I sang, and I wanted to share what I felt.

"We believe everyone has a gift for something, even if the gift is that of being a good friend. Young people should try and set a goal for themselves, and see that everything they do has some relation to the ultimate attainment of that goal. The degree with which they lend themselves to it shows the mettle of which they are made.

"The knowledge of the feelings other people have expended on me has kept me going when times were hard. That knowledge has been a responsibility, a challenge, and an inspiration. It has been the path to development and growth. The faith and confidence of others in me have been like shining, guiding stars."

Marian Anderson

BIOGRAPHICAL SKETCH

Marian Anderson grew up in a warm, close family in Philadelphia. After Marian's sixth birthday, she was enrolled in the junior choir of the church. When she was eight, her father bought an old piano, and she taught herself simple tunes. Marian was known as the "Baby Contralto," and other churches invited her to sing. Her father died during her childhood, and she earned small fees from her singing to help support her family. When she was thirteen, she was invited to join the adult choir. She learned the soprano, alto, tenor, baritone, and bass so she could substitute for anyone who was absent.

Marian had a deep, full, velvety voice with a wide range. When she registered to take voice lessons at a music school, she was turned away. The people of her church gave a concert to raise funds so that she could take singing lessons. The glorious contralto voice of this talented Black singer was first recognized in Europe, where she lived for several years. In 1935 she returned to New York and was highly acclaimed for her performance at Town Hall. In 1939, she sang at the Lincoln Memorial to 75,000 people. In 1955, she became the first Black to sing with the Metropolitan Opera company.

This great concert singer has performed at the White House, Constitution Hall, Carnegie Hall, and throughout the world. She has received honorary degrees and many other honors. The Marian Anderson Award, a scholarship fund, has been established for talented singers.

In Vienna, Arturo Toscanini, the world-famous conductor, said, "Miss Anderson, yours is a voice one hears once in a hundred years!" Perseverance, strength, courage, understanding, warmth, and reverence characterize her life. Marian Anderson has become symbolic of the fact that if a person dreams big and works hard, big dreams can come true.

CREATIVE ENCOUNTER #1..........A Class Discussion

"Listen, my child," Marian's mother said, *"whatever you do in this world, no matter how good it is, you will never be able to please everybody. All you can strive for is to do the best it is humanly possible for you to do."*

"One has to learn to take criticism, particularly the published sort, as it comes. Constructive criticism can alert a singer to bad habits in the making, and I am grateful for such comments. On the whole, however, it must be said that a serious person does not wait for the words of the critic; he checks himself. Deep in his heart he knows what his standards should be, and he strives to be faithful to them," states Marian Anderson.

What do you think about this approach to facing criticism?

Describe experiences when you were criticized.

How do you respond to criticism?

List helpful hints for dealing with criticism.

CREATIVE ENCOUNTER #2..........Musical Creative Listening

Possible selections for the following activities are: patriotic music; music by Rodgers and Hammerstein; music played by Arthur Fiedler and the Boston Pops; the "Hallelujah Chorus" by Handel; "Jesu, Joy of Man's Desiring" by Bach; "The Stars and Stripes Forever" and "Semper Fidelis" by Sousa; *The Fifth Symphony* by Beethoven; *The Grand Canyon Suite* by Grofe: "William Tell Overture" by Rossini; *Nutcracker Suite, Swan Lake, Sleeping Beauty*, and "1812" overture by Tchaikovsky.

Close your eyes. Listen creatively to the music to feel the effect it has. Visualize the music. What musical instruments do you hear? What colors and moods are portrayed in the music? What is happening in your imagination while you are listening? What is the music saying to you?

CREATIVE ENCOUNTER #3..........Musical Creative Writing

Listen to a musical selection. Write words to describe the music. Divide into groups of two or three. Using all the words you chose to describe the music and all the words the others in your group chose to describe the music, write a group composition. Share your creative writing with the other groups. This activity may be repeated with a variety of musical selections.

CREATIVE ENCOUNTER #4..........Musical Creative Drama

Try to pantomime what the music of a song might be saying. Can music portray hot, cold, darkness or light? When the music changes to a different selection, continue with your pantomime showing the change. Or begin a "second act" when the music changes.

CREATIVE ENCOUNTER #5..........Musical Creative Activities

A. **Musical Creative Spelling**

In each measure, spell words with the names of notes. Place a whole note on the lines or spaces. Be sure the notes you choose will spell a word. For example, the notes c, a, and b spell *cab*.

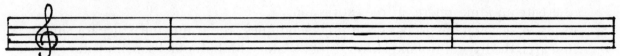

The notes in each measure spell a word. Write each word below the corresponding measure.

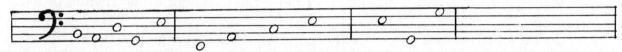

Create your own musical spelling words.

B. **Musical Creative Math**

Create musical math problems with the values of notes and rests.

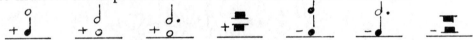

C. **Musical Creative Curiosities**

Draw a picture of an animal, design, or common object with notes, rests, bass clef, sharps, flats, and other musical notations. Display your musical creative curiosities.

D. **Announcing Analogies**

Place an X in the space beside the one correct relationship. : means "is to." :: means "as."

_____ : crescendo ::   bassoon : woodwinds ::

_____ a. # : double flat   _____ a. timpani : baroque

_____ b. D.C. : a cappella   _____ b. dolce : oratorio

_____ c. 4/4 time : metronome   _____ c. glockenspiel : percussion

_____ d. p : soft   _____ d. dulcimer : brass

E. **Secret Surprise**

1	2	3	4	5

Write the correct term on each line.
Place the first letter of each term in the corresponding blocks.

1. What is the name of this symbol? *b* _____
2. What is the synonym of forte? _____
3. What is a four-stringed Hawaiian instrument of the guitar family? _____
4. What is the name of this symbol?

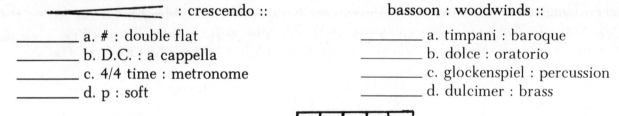

5. What is the name of this note? _____

INDEPENDENT PROJECTS—ANDERSON

1. Study music theory and musical terms.
2. Devise new creative activities to learn music theory.
3. Compose your own songs.
4. Blend music and words through creative experimentation. While dramatically speaking, play different kinds of background music. Adjust the volume of the music to create an atmosphere of free expression.
5. Practice, develop the proper breathing techniques, and train your voice for singing.
6. Research the lives of Roland Hayes, Ethel Waters, Mahalia Jackson, and other Black musicians.
7. While listening to music:
   a. Create a puppet show, or move the puppets to the rhythm of music.
   b. Write your name with a flashlight, or move the flashlight to the rhythm of the music.
   c. Create actions to songs. Describe the music with sign language or actions to someone who cannot hear.
   d. Paint your interpretations of the music.
   e. Design a creative drawing. Draw the lines upward when the notes ascend. Draw the lines downward when the notes descend.

RESOURCE BOOKS—ANDERSON

Anderson, Marian. *My Lord, What a Morning.* New York: The Viking Press, 1956.

Hughes, Langston. *Famous Negro Music Makers.* New York: Dodd, Mead & Co., 1955.

Lloyd, Norman. *The Golden Encyclopedia of Music.* New York: Golden Press, 1968.

Newman, Shirlee P. *Marian Anderson: Lady from Philadelphia.* Philadelphia: The Westminster Press, 1966.

Stevenson, Janet. *Singing to the World: Marian Anderson.* Chicago: Encyclopaedia Britannica Press, Inc., 1963.

Tobias, Tobi. *Marian Anderson.* New York: Thomas Y. Crowell Co., 1972.

MARY KAY ASH

"At Mary Kay, our philosophy rests on three beautiful ideas. The first, and most important, is the golden rule. We teach our people to treat other people as they would like to be treated. Sometimes we call this our Go-Give spirit, and we give special recognition to those who show that spirit in outstanding ways. It's a spirit of sharing and caring for the other person.

"The second cornerstone of our philosophy is our belief in the right priorities: God first, family second, career third.

"Our third cornerstone is our belief in the beautiful potential inside every human being. We believe that everyone can be successful, with enough encouragement and praise."

Mary Kay

BIOGRAPHICAL SKETCH

The words of Mary Kay's mother became the theme of her childhood, and they have stayed with Mary Kay all her life: *"You can do it."* The confidence her mother instilled in Mary Kay has been a tremendous help and influence; *"You can do it!"* is the daily theme at Mary Kay Cosmetics. Due to her father's illness, Mary Kay's mother was the sole support of the family, which made it necessary for Mary Kay from the age of seven to have many responsibilities at home.

Competing and striving to excel was fun for her, and she was willing to make sacrifices and work hard to achieve success. Mary Kay enjoyed the satisfaction of bringing home A's, and in junior high school she discovered her talents of typing, extemporaneous speaking, and debating.

After working in the direct-sales field for over twenty-five years, she decided to retire in 1963. She compiled all the direct-selling techniques that she had learned over the years. The product philosophy of Mary Kay Cosmetics was inspired by a hide tanner's concept. The original sales organization included Mary Kay herself and nine independent beauty consultants.

Since Mary Kay Cosmetics was founded in 1963, the company has grown dramatically to achieve international prominence. The company's international headquarters in Dallas is housed in a high-rise tower that stands as a symbol of achievement. Thousands of prizes are awarded to her consultants ranging from keys to pink cadillacs to diamond bumblebees. Mary Kay Cosmetics has been recognized nationally in editorials appearing in leading business, women's and fashion magazines, as well as *Reader's Digest* and the CBS News show *60 Minutes*.

For Mary Kay, the most meaningful aspect of the growth of the company has been seeing so many women achieve. Mary Kay says that a woman often comes into the company like a tight little rosebud, and with praise and encouragement she changes into a beautiful rose, poised and confident. Mary Kay is convinced that competition is most productive when you are competing with yourself. Her formula for happiness is a job you love, people you care about, and something to look forward to. Mary Kay has given opportunities to thousands of women, and her enthusiasm inspires them to dream big, set goals, and turn ambitions into realities.

CREATIVE ENCOUNTER #1.........Creative Drama

*"I really believe that if you **act** enthusiastic, you will **become** enthusiastic! Not just for a day but for a lifetime!*

*"You **can** do things to make yourself enthusiastic. It's interesting to note that the word **enthusiasm** comes from a Greek word meaning 'God within.' Enthusiasm is a great advantage in anything you do—and certainly in sales. I'm sure my own enthusiasm was my number one asset when I first got into sales."*

Describe a situation when your enthusiasm helped you to achieve. When has your contagious enthusiasm influenced others?

What steps can you take to become more enthusiastic?

Role play the following situation: Your friend is discouraged and does not think he can achieve his goal. He has been working hard for many weeks to finish his project, and now he is facing difficult setbacks. Ask your friend what goal he is trying to reach. Share your "I can" attitude and enthusiasm with your friend.

CREATIVE ENCOUNTER #2.........A Brainstorming Session

Brainstorm: Make a list of all the jobs you can think of that have been generated by the Mary Kay Company. A few of these jobs include consultants, automobile manufacturers, publishers for Mary Kay's autobiography, and computer technologists.

Choose a product: grandfather clock, jet, bicycle, toy, light bulb, football, etc.

Brainstorm: List all jobs that are involved in the production and marketing of that product.

CREATIVE ENCOUNTER #3.........Setting Goals

*"I believe it's important to commit your goals to writing. It's also important to limit your list to just **six items.** Don't be overzealous and put down seventeen. If you do, you'll start to think, 'I can't possibly do all this.' You'll be so overwhelmed that you'll end up not getting anything done. If you can accomplish those six things, you've accomplished a lot.*

"I realized that the real thrill was in being able to do the work I loved. Even today, I get up at five and start on my list of the 'six most important things I must do today.' I love the sense of accomplishment that I feel when at the end of the day that list is completed."

Keep a list of six things you need to accomplish daily.

Do the most important task first and the rest in the order of their importance. Tell someone to remind and encourage you to complete your tasks. Race with the clock or yourself; set a time limit and try to get the job done in that amount of time. Reward yourself after you've finished your tasks.

CREATIVE ENCOUNTER #4.........Time Management

"Time is just too precious to be wasted. If I were to name one quality necessary for success in sales, it would have to be good time management."

Carry a calendar with you. Write reminders ahead in your calendar. Evaluate how you are using your time. Make a list of ways you can manage your time more effectively and wisely. Design your own calendar with illustrations and your goals. Set your annual, monthly, weekly, and daily goals. List the steps to help you reach your goals. Include time for family, friends, studies, school projects, jobs, leisure, and extracurricular activities.

CREATIVE ENCOUNTER #5..........Improving Listening Skills

"As things turned out, people have stood in lines to shake my hand, and I have always tried my best to make every single person feel important. People have asked me, 'How do you do it? Aren't you exhausted?' Of course, but I do it because I know how it feels to be brushed off by somebody who's important to you. And whether you're standing in a reception line or talking to your child after school, it's always important to focus all your attention on the person in front of you. If you can love that person, that's all the better. But you must never treat anyone in a way you wouldn't like to be treated yourself."

Listen with care and empathy. Accept the other as a worthy person. Help clarify the other person's feelings. Be aware of eye contact. Silence can be valuable in a conversation. A speaker notices his audience. Be an active listener as a member of an audience, also.

You are telling someone your thoughts. How do you want him/her to listen to you?

Brainstorm: What are characteristics of a good listener?

Divide into groups of two. One student states thoughts, problems, or ideas. The partner responds to restate the message in other words to help understand the meaning. Reflect remarks with "You think . . . ." "It seems to you that . . . ." "You mean you feel . . . ." "Do I hear you saying . . . ." Change roles.

An example is the following:

Statement: "I'm determined to get good grades."

Paraphrased Response: "You see yourself as an ambitious student."

Ask your students questions similar to those below and have them answer with yes, no, sometimes, or I am improving.

Do I listen creatively?

Do I listen to other people's feelings?

Do I listen closely to help understand the meaning of the message?

Do I listen and speak with courtesy?

Do I look directly at the other person?

Do I look for others' contributions rather than being so involved with my own?

When I disagree, do I disagree pleasantly?

Do I listen with care?

How can I continue to improve my listening skills?

"I find that if you must criticize, it's best to sandwich it between two thick layers of praise, and just barely mention the criticism.

*"One of my favorite expressions is, 'We fail forward to success.' You **will** make mistakes and sometimes you'll be frustrated in trying to meet your goals. But for every failure, there's an alternative. Have confidence in yourself, and you'll find another route. Remember obstacles either 'polish us up' or 'wear us down.' A diamond was once just a hunk of coal until it was put under pressure, then polished to perfection."*

Problem Focus: Identify the problem, goal, or challenge. Each person in the circle completes the question, "How can I . . . ?" Choose the "How can I . . . ?" that will be discussed today. Some examples could be the following: How can I achieve this goal? How can I get my work done? How can I consistently practice piano, sports, etc? How can I help solve the problems on the playground? How can I earn and save money? How can I keep my room clean?

Relational Stage: Ask questions to clarify the problem, goal, or challenge. This will help to understand that others may have similar concerns.

Alternative Stage: Members of your group may offer suggestions for achieving this goal or solving this problem. Little or no evaluation should take place during this stage. Someone may record these suggestions on the board. Choose an alternative. What can you do to begin to achieve your goal this week?

Follow-up Session: At the next session report how you have begun to solve this problem, goal, or challenge.

Try to recognize and express your own views and feelings. Use this technique in situations that arise in your daily lives.

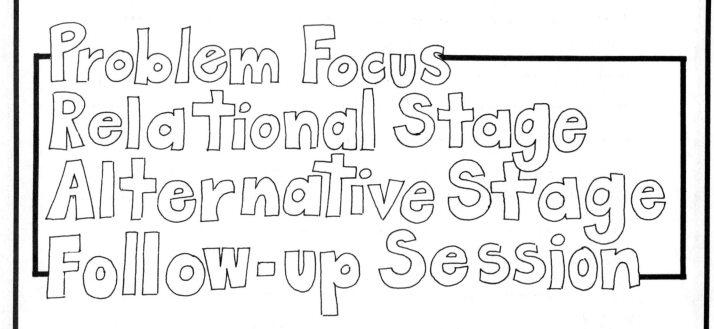

Problem Focus
Relational Stage
Alternative Stage
Follow-up Session

The instructions for the Child Study Technique are adapted from Dr. Dorothy Sisk of the University of South Florida in Tampa.

CREATIVE ENCOUNTER #7.........Solving Problems

Answer each of the following questions in a way that will help you meet your goals and identify your problems.

1. Identify the problem, goal, or challenge.

   How can I _____?

2. Ask questions to clarify the problem, goal, or challenge.

   _____

   _____

3. Offer suggestions for achieving this goal or solving this problem.

   _____

   _____

4. What can you do to begin to achieve your goal this week?

   _____

   _____

   _____

5. After you have taken the first steps in solving your problem, write about your progress.

   _____

   _____

   _____

   _____

6. What is the outcome of your problem? _____

   _____

   _____

   _____

Solving Problems

CREATIVE ENCOUNTER #8.........The "I Can" Attitude

The bumblebee is the symbol of Mary Kay Cosmetics. Aerodynamic engineers have proven that it is impossible for the bumblebee to fly. The body is too heavy, and the wings are too weak. However, the bumblebee does not know that and flies, works, and achieves. Mary Kay believes her consultants have found their wings and are flying just like the bumblebee. Mary Kay teaches her consultants to throw negative thoughts away and replace them with *"I can, I will, I must!"* Some people told Mary Kay it was impossible to start her business, but others encouraged her: *"You can do it!"* So she did.

Believe in yourself. Accomplish your goals by believing *"I can,"* no matter how difficult the goals, handicaps, or stumbling blocks. How does the lesson of the bumblebee apply to you?

Work on changing your attitude to *"I can."* Make a list of your goals, beginning each goal with *"I can."*

1. I can _____
2. I can _____
3. I can _____
4. I can _____
5. I can _____
6. I can _____

Draw an illustration to represent the concept *"I can."* Write the words *"I can!"* and *"I can, if I think I can!"* on your illustration. Place this little reminder of your great potential where it will encourage you every day.

CREATIVE ENCOUNTER #9..........Designing a Product

You are an executive in a growing business. It is your responsibility to design a new product. Let your imagination soar. Your product will affect the lives of many people.

1. Draw an illustration of your product in the space below.

2. Write an advertisement about your product. Convince others of the importance of your product. Include instructions on how to use your product.

_____

_____

_____

_____

_____

_____

_____

_____

_____

_____

_____

_____

_____

_____

INDEPENDENT PROJECTS—ASH

1. Invite a Mary Kay Beauty Consultant from your community to demonstrate and teach skin care techniques. Ask her to tell about the training programs, Mary Kay Cosmetics' annual seminar in Dallas, Texas, and the Mary Kay enthusiasm, songs, and philosophy.

2. Express your thoughts on these topics in a speech and/or creative writing: the "I can" attitude, self-confidence, enthusiasm, dreams and goals, praise and criticism, determination, success and failure, competition, time and money management, motivation, the Go-Give spirit, and a formula for happiness.

3. Organize a business. Select the executives for the company and delegate responsibilities. Describe your business, the need for your product or service, labor, sales, and records.

4. Design a billboard and plan a radio or television advertisement for your product or business. Tape-record or videotape your advertisement.

5. Brainstorm: List all the ways you can think of to earn money. Use your creativity to think of new ways to utilize your abilities and to offer them to other people. Give lessons to younger children. Read, bake, run errands, or play your musical instrument for shut-ins. Other opportunities include garden and lawn care, farm work, and apprenticeships.

6. If you had $1,000, how would you spend it? Plan a budget for your money.

7. Keep a record of how much money you gave to worthy causes, how much you saved, and how much you spent for a week. Are you pleased with how you spent your money? What changes do you need to make in your spending habits?

RESOURCE BOOKS—ASH

Ash, Mary Kay. *Mary Kay.* New York: Harper & Row, Publishers, 1981.

Caney, Steven. *Steven Caney's Kids' America.* New York: Workman Publishing Co., Inc., 1978.

Foder, R.V. *Nickels, Dimes, and Dollars: How Currency Works.* New York: William Morrow and Co., 1980.

Hoag, Edwin. *How Business Works.* New York: The Bobbs-Merrill Co., Inc., 1978.

Holz, Loretta. *Make It and Sell It: A Young People's Guide to Marketing Crafts.* New York: Charles Scribner's Sons, 1978.

How Things Are Made. Washington, D.C.: The National Geographic Society, 1981.

James, Elizabeth, and Carol Barkin. *How to Grow a Hundred Dollars.* New York: Lothrop, Lee & Shepard Co., 1979.

Lee, Mary Price. *Money and Kids: How to Earn It, Save It, and Spend It.* Philadelphia: Westminster Press, 1973.

Sattler, Helen Roney. *Dollars from Dandelions: 101 Ways to Earn Money.* New York: Lothrop, Lee & Shepard Co., 1979.

Seuling, Barbara. *You Can't Count a Billion Dollars & Other Little-Known Facts About Money.* Garden City, New York: Doubleday & Co., Inc., 1979.

JOHN JAMES AUDUBON

"I never for a day gave up listening to the songs of birds or watching their ways or drawing them in the best way I could. During my deepest troubles I would often take myself away from the people around me and return to some hidden part of the forest to listen to the wood thrush's melodies.

"Ah, my dear friend, would that you were here just now to see the Snipes innumerable, the Blackbirds, the Gallinules, and the Curlews that surround us;—that you could listen as I now do, to the delightful notes of the Mockingbird, pouring forth his soul in melody as the glorious orb of day is fast descending towards the western horizon;—that you could gaze on the Great Herons which, after spreading their broad wings, croak aloud as if doubtful regarding the purpose of our visit to these shores!"

John J. Audubon

BIOGRAPHICAL SKETCH

From early childhood John James Audubon began to draw, study, and observe birds. Instead of going to school, he usually spent the day searching for birds' nests, fishing, or shooting. When his father, a sea captain, returned from one of his frequent sea journeys, he realized his son was not progressing in his studies at school. His father made no comment, but early the next morning he took his son in a private carriage on a journey to a naval base, where he was enrolled in a military academy. However, Audubon soon returned to his home and school. His father gave up steering his son toward a naval career, for he recognized and encouraged his son's artistic ability.

Traveling across America in his search for birds, this explorer and skilled hunter faced frontier dangers. He showed perseverance in the face of many setbacks, including financial difficulties. He left a portfolio of nearly 1,000 valuable drawings with a relative. After he discovered that his treasure had become a home for rats, he was very disheartened. However, this woodsman took his gun, notebook, and pencils and journeyed to the woods as if nothing had happened. He felt pleased that now he would make much better drawings than before, and within three years he had a portfolio filled again.

Unable to find a publisher for his paintings in the United States, Audubon went to England in 1826. There he sold enough subscriptions to publish his work. The first volume of *Birds of America* was published in 1827. The novelty of his style of drawing birds in action brought him fame and fortune. Audubon returned to the United States in 1839 and published American editions of his artwork. He became prosperous and continued his paintings on expeditions across America. The complete edition of *Birds of America* contained 435 hand-colored plates with 1,065 life-size figures of American birds in their natural surroundings. Descriptions of these birds appeared later in *Ornithological Biography*. His last project was a two-volume book of mammals called *Viviparous Quadrupeds of North America*.

John James Audubon had a tremendous love, fascination, and talent for his work. He is an outstanding example of the success that comes from determination and enthusiasm. Curiosity, independence, and abundant energy were characteristics displayed in fulfilling his task of making and publishing his own drawings of the birds of America. The National Audubon Society makes the work of John James Audubon, naturalist, artist, and ornithologist, live on.

CREATIVE ENCOUNTER #1.........Creative Art

During his childhood, John James Audubon carried his little basket filled with food to the woods. When he returned home, the basket was replenished with what he called "curiosities," such as birds' nests, birds' eggs, lichens, flowers, and pebbles. Collect these materials of nature on a hike: cornhusks, seed corn, corncobs, ears of corn, corn silk, pinecones, acorns, nuts, milkweeds, feathers, stones, leaves, and shells. Provide scraps of cloth, yarn, felt, egg cartons, pipe cleaners, pompons, string, rubber bands, safety pins, scissors, needles, and thread.

Create a variety of "creative curiosities."

Examples: a doll and a plane from cornhusks; a scarecrow, a rocket, and a boat from corncobs; a wreath from a braided cornhusk; an owl, a turkey, and a rabbit from pinecones; a parakeet from a milkweed; a mouse from a walnut with a braided cornhusk for the tail; a painted turtle from a rock; and a raccoon from pompons and seed corn.

Hints: Soak the cornhusks for about three minutes in lukewarm water. While the cornhusks are wet and flexible, cut, shape, roll, curl, braid, and work with the cornhusks. Seed corn can be used for eyes or a nose.

CREATIVE ENCOUNTER #2.........Creative Drawings

Sketch drawings similar to the artwork of John James Audubon. Use your choice of medium: pencils, colored pencils, pastels, watercolors, or crayons. Use these drawings of nature, birds, and animals as a background in a diorama, mural, or display for your "creative curiosities."

Trace the shape of your state, and draw a picture with this shape. Add details to the shape of your state to disguise it.

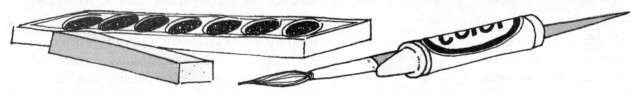

CREATIVE ENCOUNTER #3.........Following Directions

Divide into groups of two. Arrange your chairs back to back. Draw an animal, design, or common object. Describe what you have drawn to your partner. Following your directions, your partner will try to sketch your drawing. Your partner does not look at your drawing. After completion, compare your drawing with your partner's drawing. Are your drawings similar? How can you improve your directions? Change roles. Try one-way communication: Your partner may not ask questions while you are drawing and giving directions.

Then with another drawing, try two-way communication in which your partner may ask questions.

Share your drawings with the group.

CREATIVE ENCOUNTER #4..........A Creative Illustration

John James Audubon successfully developed and used his talents. Think about these questions: What are your talents? How can you use these talents? Write down specific talents, characteristics, and interests and try to become more aware of them. This will help you view yourself differently.

Example: I am like a kitten because I am curious, fun, and energetic.

1. What kind of animal are you like? _____

   Why? _____

   _____

2. What kind of bird are you like? _____

   Why? _____

   _____

3. What kind of fish are you like? _____

   Why? _____

   _____

4. What kind of weather are you like? _____

   Why? _____

   _____

5. What kind of fruit or vegetable are you like? _____

   Why? _____

   _____

6. What kind of plant or tree are you like? _____

   Why? _____

   _____

7. What kind of flower are you like? _____

   Why? _____

   _____

Put together parts of the animal, bird, fish, weather, fruit, vegetable, plant, tree, and flower that you are like to form a fun and creative illustration of yourself.

After completion, share your drawings. Try to find the animal, bird, fish, and the other representations in each other's drawings.

INDEPENDENT PROJECTS—AUDUBON

1. Study the artistic styles and techniques of John James Audubon and other artists. Find out what tools and media they used.
2. Make a portfolio of your own sketches of animals and birds in their natural habitats.
3. Conduct a nature study, hike, and nature treasure hunt. Take your sketch pad and camera. Focus on your five senses and your keen ability to observe.
4. Sketch animal tracks on charts.
5. Tape the sounds of nature for your friends. Have them listen to the recording and identify the sounds.
6. Compile a fact file about the size, sounds, actions, characteristics, living habits, and the environments of animals and birds.
7. Display your collections of rocks, plants, flowers, seeds, shells, insects, or butterflies.
8. Prepare and conduct tree tours to share your research about trees and nature with younger children.
9. Create a story, poem, or painting to tell about unusual events that the trees might have witnessed during their lifetimes.
10. Write or print your name in as many different ways as possible. Make a design with your name.
11. Glue a picture of a tree, bicycle, scenery, or other illustration to a paper. Add imaginative details to the picture.
12. What are things you could make from an egg carton? Brainstorm a list to demonstrate that there are many possibilities for using an ordinary object.

RESOURCE BOOKS—AUDUBON

Audubon, John James. *Birds of America*. New York: The Macmillan Co., 1937.

Brenner, Barbara. *On the Frontier with Mr. Audubon*. New York: Coward, McCann & Geoghegan, Inc., 1977.

Doeser, Linda, ed. *The World's Wildlife in Color*. Secaucus, N.J.: Castle Books, 1975.

Emberley, Rebecca. *Drawing with Numbers and Letters*. Boston: Little, Brown and Co., 1981.

Fisher, Clyde. *The Life of Audubon*. New York: Harper and Brothers, Publishers, 1949.

Ford, Alice, ed. *Audubon's Animals: The Quadrupeds of North America*. New York: The Studio Publications, Inc., 1951.

Hochman, Shirley. *Invitation to Art*. New York: Sterling Publishing Co., Inc., 1974.

Howard, Joan. *The Story of John J. Audubon*. New York: Grosset & Dunlap, 1954.

Kieran, Margaret and John. *John James Audubon*. New York: Random House, Inc., 1954.

Mason, Miriam E. *Young Audubon: Boy Naturalist*. New York: The Bobbs-Merrill Co., 1943.

Peattie, Donald Culross, ed. *Audubon's America: The Narratives and Experiences of John James Audubon*. Boston: Houghton Mifflin Co., 1940.

Rourke, Constance. *Audubon*. New York: Franklin Watts, Inc., 1964.

Terres, John K., ed. *The Audubon Book of True Nature Stories*. New York: Thomas Y. Crowell Co., 1958.

Zaidenberg, Arthur. *How to Paint with Water Colors: A Book for Beginners*. New York: The Vanguard Press, Inc., 1968.

SAMUEL BUTCHER

"I call the little figurines my little messengers. I use the verses in Precious Moments to reach the hearts of people.

"Many times people ask if I paint from models. No, I don't. But I do paint from the soul and spirit of that person. That really becomes a model. When I meet a particular individual and that character stands out to me, that character becomes my model many, many times in my art-work.

"I'm sure that if I live to be 300 years old, I would never run out of subject matter, because there's so many things that God has been gracious enough to bring into our lives, that we can impart the things that He's done for us, to share it with people so that they might also be comforted.

"Art to us is our hobby. It is our vocation. It is our very life, because it represents a God that is so much a part of us."

BIOGRAPHICAL SKETCH

Samuel Butcher was recognized as an artist from a very young age. He was raised in a family of hot rod, race car, and motorcycle drivers. All the children were involved except Sam, and he was different. Teachers would often write letters to his parents and tell them about Sam's talent. But his family had little regard for the art world and did not appreciate their son's unusual gift.

After receiving a scholarship in 1958, Sam attended the College of Arts and Crafts in Berkeley, California. He took fine art and educational classes, intending to become an instructor of advanced painting and art history on the secondary level. Sam was an illustrator in an international organization for about five years and then became a teacher of teachers for the same firm, as well as a storyteller for children on a national television program.

Sam had worked for the company for four years when he met William Biele, who later became his business partner and best friend. After working together for about two years, they decided to form their own greeting card company, which they named Jonathan & David, Inc. They took many free-lance jobs illustrating for large publishing companies, when Bill encouraged Sam to develop the artwork that is so popular today, which is known as the Precious Moments line. They showed the line at the Christian Booksellers Association in Anaheim, California, where it received immediate recognition.

After Precious Moments had been on the market for two years, Sam and Bill were contacted by Mr. Gene Friedman, president of Enesco Imports, who asked if they would be interested in licensing the products in fine porcelain bisque. Since that time, Precious Moments has found itself in other products, such as counted cross-stitch, crewel, glassware of many kinds, dolls, children's clothing, and candles.

Sam is not only an illustrator of the sensitive Precious Moments children but enjoys nonobjective and abstract expressionism. He is interested in creative writing and teaching, as well as art. His wife, Katie, is also a very fine artist and a designer of clothing for the Precious Moments dolls. Sam and Katie live with three of their seven children on a little farm in Missouri and are the proud grandparents of five "precious" grandchildren.

23

CREATIVE ENCOUNTER #1..........Designing a Card

Imagine that your best friend breaks his/her leg and is confined to a hospital for a short stay. You decide to make your own greeting card to send to cheer him/her up.

Design the card that you would like to send.

a. Front of Card

b. Inside of Card

CREATIVE ENCOUNTER #2..........Birthday Greetings

Someone who means a great deal to you is celebrating a birthday next week. You want to let him/her know that he/she is a very special person, and none of the greeting cards you've looked at seem appropriate. You are determined to make your own card and write a verse that will convey your feelings regarding this person.

Compose your verse on the simulated card below.

(Inside of Card)

CREATIVE ENCOUNTER #3..........Expressing Feelings

Artists express their feelings about everyday occurrences, events, and people. Often the expression of their feelings comes out in some kind of art form.

What kinds of feelings or emotions do you sometimes have?

The facial expression on each drawing below might typify the kind of feeling the character is expressing.

a. Happy   b. Angry   c. Sad   d. Confused

Think of some other emotions. How would you depict them?

Write the name of the emotion in the blank below each of the faces and draw the corresponding features.

_____   _____   _____   _____

1. What is your most precious moment? _____

_____

2. What is your funniest moment? _____

_____

3. What is your most embarrassing moment? _____

_____

4. What is your happiest moment? _____

_____

CREATIVE ENCOUNTER #4.........Precious Moments

When Sam was in kindergarten, he illustrated a story on a roll of paper and made his own little movie. As a kindergartener, he was invited to present his movie to the other classrooms from the first through the sixth grade. When Sam was in the fourth grade, several classes were consolidated to do a stage production of *The Ugly Duckling*, and he did all the backdrops and costumes for the play.

Sometimes other people can help you identify your abilities and strengths by commenting that you do well in certain areas.

1. What are your special talents? _____

   _____

2. In what ways have you shared your talents? _____

   _____

   _____

   _____

Try to think of the Precious Moments in your life, for example, times you spend with your family, friends, and doing things that you enjoy. Identify those Precious Moments below. Some examples could be the following:

A Precious Moment is spending time with a friend.

A Precious Moment is smelling freshly baked cookies in Mom's kitchen.

A Precious Moment is _____

A Precious Moment is _____

A Precious Moment is _____

Lines are the basis for cartoons. Stretch your imagination and add details to each of the drawings below to illustrate Precious Moments in your life.

Drop
everything

What a joy

Precious moments

The illustrations on this page and page 29 are examples of Sam Butcher's *Precious Moments*. These illustrations can be used to add direction to many of the Creative Encounters and Independent Projects presented in this unit.

Give a little whistle

Let's keep in touch

"The eyes really draw you to the figurines because they are very large and very sensitive. If you're standing twenty feet away from a piece of porcelain, what you see are little eyes that appear to be so sad that they are going to cry. But if you continue to walk toward the figurine, all of a sudden those eyes begin to smile, because the smile on the face isn't shown from twenty feet away. But it begins to appear on the face as you get closer. You are looking at something that looked sad, then begins to smile, and it is a living thing."

To God be the glory

INDEPENDENT PROJECTS—BUTCHER

1. Collect quotations of famous Americans and compile a book of these inspirational quotations. Make bookmarks or greeting cards to encourage your family and friends by writing these quotations in calligraphy.

2. Design and create a stage with sets and props for puppets or stuffed animals, using a shoe box or similar container plus a variety of ordinary household materials. Write a short script for the play using your characters. Go into production for your friends, family, or class at school.

3. Create a "touch and feel" book for a young child, utilizing materials at hand. You may want to substitute cotton balls for lambs, toothpicks for fence posts, scraps of material for clothing, etc. Create a simple story and illustrate it with "touch and feel" effects glued to the scenes.

4. Make your own old-time movie. Draw a cartoon character or animal on the pages of a small blank note pad or plain paper squares stapled together along the top. With the advance of each paper, slightly move the character's position in your drawing a little at a time. Turn the pages of your booklet rapidly in succession and watch the animated effect, which simulates an old-time "flick" movie.

5. Draw a detailed illustration with hidden objects in it. Create a maze. Present these projects to your friends to solve.

6. Create your own figurines from clay.

7. Collect cartoons and pictures in magazines. Make up captions for these pictures.

RESOURCE BOOKS—BUTCHER

Buechner, Thomas S. *Norman Rockwell: A Sixty Year Retrospective.* New York: Harry N. Abrams, Inc., 1972.

Enesco Precious Moments Collections: Official Collectors' Illustrated Guide. Chicago: Enesco Imports Corporation and Enesco Precious Moments Collectors' Club, 1983.

Finch, Christopher. *Norman Rockwell's America.* New York: Harry N. Abrams, Inc., 1975.

Guptill, Arthur L. *Norman Rockwell: Illustrator.* New York: Watson-Guptill Publications, 1946.

Hotchkiss, John F. *Hummel Art.* Des Moines, Iowa: Wallace-Homestead Book Company, 1978.

Mendelson, Lee, and Charles M. Schulz. *Happy Birthday, Charlie Brown.* New York: Random House, Inc., 1979.

Nussbaum, Hedda, ed. *Charlie Brown's Fourth Super Book of Questions and Answers About All Kinds of People and How They Live!* New York: Random House, Inc., 1979.

Rockwell, Norman. *My Adventures as an Illustrator.* Garden City, New York: Doubleday & Co., Inc., 1960.

Schulz, Charles M. *Peanuts Jubilee: My Life and Art with Charlie Brown and Others.* New York: Holt, Rinehart and Winston, 1975.

Schulz, Charles M. *Peanuts Treasury.* New York: Holt, Rinehart and Winston, 1968.

Zaidenberg, Arthur. *How to Draw Cartoons! A Beginner's Book for Young People.* New York: The Vanguard Press, Inc., 1959.

GEORGE WASHINGTON CARVER

"Back of my workshop there is a little grove of trees. One has been cut down. It makes a good seat. I have made it a rule to go out and sit on it at 4 o'clock every morning and ask the good Lord what I am to do that day. Then I go ahead and do it.

"Alone there with the things I love most, I gather my specimens and study the lessons Nature is so eager to teach us all. Nothing is more beautiful than the loveliness of the woods before sunrise.

"God is going to reveal things to us that He never revealed before if we put our hand in His. The thing that I am to do and the way of doing it come to me. I never have to grope for methods; the method is revealed at the moment I am inspired to create something new. Without God to draw aside the curtain I would be helpless."

G. W. Carver.

BIOGRAPHICAL SKETCH

George was born into slavery on a plantation in Missouri in the midst of the Civil War. His parents were slaves of Moses Carver. Soon after George was born, his father died. A few months later George was kidnapped with his mother by thieving night riders. Moses Carver bartered his racehorse to recover the sickly infant. But his mother was never found, so the Carvers raised George themselves.

Early in his childhood, George had a keen interest in nature, health, and nutrition. He was a shy and gentle child with an insatiable quest for learning. There were no schools for Negro children near his home. So at the age of ten, he left home seeking an education. He went from place to place doing all kinds of work to pay for his schooling.

George first studied art at Simpson College in Iowa. In 1894 he graduated from Iowa State College of Agricultural and Mechanical Arts. At the invitation of Booker T. Washington, he joined the staff at Tuskegee Institute as the head of the Department of Agriculture in 1896. He spent the rest of his life there.

George W. Carver saw the South as a land of abundance if only men could learn to use its rich resources wisely. One of Dr. Carver's goals was to preserve the small family farm. He believed the results of research must be brought directly into the lives of the people. Thus, he traveled through the South with his scientific exhibits to demonstrate techniques to improve farming.

Dr. Carver gave advice freely to those who consulted him. When his students were suffering from the hurts of discrimination and prejudice, they sought Dr. Carver's counsel. He instilled in each student pride in his ability and the desire to extend it.

Dr. Carver was awarded honorary degrees, medals, and citations for his achievements in the advancement of chemurgy and for his contributions to the health and living conditions of the people living in the South. From "God's Little Workshop," the name of Dr. Carver's laboratory, came discoveries that enriched America and the world. His epitaph stated, "He could have added fortune to fame, but caring for neither, he found happiness and honor in being helpful to the world."

CREATIVE ENCOUNTER #1.........A Class Discussion

"Life requires thorough preparation," stated Dr. Carver. He taught his students to learn to respect themselves and others and to be the best they could be. Dr. Carver had many talents. Early in his childhood, he learned to cook, wash, clean, iron, knit, and crochet. He did outstanding work in his college courses of botany, chemistry, zoology, bacteriology, geology, and entomology. He was skilled with his hands, and he was a remarkable artist, pianist, and vocalist.

What new skill would you like to develop?

What are some ways to show respect for people?

Dr. Carver inspired his students to do ordinary tasks in new, innovative ways.

Brainstorm: What are all the ways that you can think of to move a heavy object?

His philosophy was to start where you are, with what you have, and make something from it. He did not have the necessary equipment for his agricultural laboratory at Tuskegee, so he devised his own. What common objects would you use to make science equipment?

CREATIVE ENCOUNTER #2.........A Creative Scientist

"I therefore went on to try different combinations of the parts under different conditions of temperatures and pressure and the result is what you see."

Dr. Carver developed over 300 products from the peanut and over 100 products from the sweet potato. Become a creative scientist. Investigate the products and results of Dr. Carver's creative scientific research.

What are various products that are derived from the peanut, sweet potato, and other sources?

_____ _____

_____ _____

_____ _____

_____ _____

_____ _____

CREATIVE ENCOUNTER #3..........A Creative Cook

You have become a business partner of the Peanut Palace. Your restaurant is known for its nutritious, delicious meals. Your specialities are Dr. Carver's recipes for dandelion salad and English peanut bread. Peanut butter can be used as an ingredient in cake, cookies, and sandwiches or served on celery.

Think of a variety of ways to use the peanut in your restaurant.

Become a creative cook. Investigate recipes and cooking techniques.

Think of creative names for your salads and other dishes.

Plan and design a menu and an advertisement for the Peanut Palace.

Menus

CREATIVE ENCOUNTER #4..........Designing a Park

When George W. Carver was very young, plants became his toys. He had a secret garden to nurture sick plants, and he became known as the "Plant Doctor." Dr. Carver believed that every child should be involved in the study of nature and agriculture.

Refer to a variety of resource books about the study of nature, gardening, and wildlife. Design a park that will offer nature study and recreation for people of all ages. Plan for gardens, greenhouses, trails for nature hikes, playground, ski resort, pond, animal refuge, an aquarium, a solar-heated museum, and laboratory. Label the names of the trees, flowers, and plants in your park.

Design creative playground equipment for your park.

Display your drawing of the park.

A Sketch of My Park

While the introduction is being read, close your eyes and think about being an animal. Become an animal in your imagination. Respond to the questions as though you are an animal.

Imagine yourself wandering in a meadow. Take time to smell the beautiful flowers. Observe the splendid array of the colors of nature. Feel the warmth of the sunshine. As you wade across a clear, rippling stream, you curiously spot your image in the water. You are approaching majestic mountains and a vast forest of trees gently swaying in the breeze. The wondrous sights, sounds, and scents of wildlife surround you. Reach out and touch the beauty of nature.

1. What kind of animal are you?
2. Your favorite place in the forest has a captivating view. Tell about this hideaway.
3. The animal friends are together. Tell us about your life, your family, and home in the forest.
4. Tell us about an adventure at the time of the sunrise or sunset or during the spring, summer, autumn, or winter.
5. A squirrel is chattering. What is the exciting news?
6. Mysterious tracks! Who made these tracks?
7. A fire! How will you organize the animals to work as a team to extinguish the fire?
8. You are peeking around a tree, inquisitively watching the visitors. If you could talk to people, what would you tell them?
9. You and your animal friends have enjoyed a life of freedom, roaming, and blue skies. However, you have also encountered dangers and the turbulence of storms. How have you helped other animal friends?

INDEPENDENT PROJECTS—CARVER

1. Plan a documentary about wildlife, forestry, forest products, and the careers of forest rangers.
2. Create an imaginary skit about the day you talked to animals.
3. Make a chart of the functions and sources of vitamins.
4. Read the labels on food and analyze the value of the food you eat.
5. Make a poster about the uses of the aloe vera plant.
6. Write a pamphlet about the uses of herbs, such as dandelion root, alfalfa, peppermint, and yarrow.
7. Set up a terrarium and an aquarium.
8. Research topics in the fields of agriculture, horticulture, botany, chemurgy, geology, zoology, or herpetology.
9. Conduct creative science experiments.
10. Develop your skills in nature photography.
11. Visit a farm, greenhouse, or state park. Record your observations in a nature diary.

RESOURCE BOOKS—CARVER

Cobb, Vicki. *More Science Experiments You Can Eat.* New York: J.B. Lippincott, 1979.

DeBruin, Jerry. *Creative, Hands-On Science Experiences: Using Free and Inexpensive Materials.* Carthage, Illinois: Good Apple, Inc., 1980.

Elliot, Lawrence. *George Washington Carver: The Man Who Overcame.* Englewood Cliffs, New Jersey: Prentice-Hall, Inc., 1966.

Goldstein-Jackson, Kevin, Norman Rudnick, and Ronald Hyman. *Experiments with Everyday Objects: Science Activities for Children, Parents, and Teachers.* Englewood Cliffs, New Jersey: Prentice-Hall, Inc., 1978.

Graham, Shirley, and George D. Lipscomb. *Dr. George Washington Carver: Scientist.* New York: Julian Messner, Inc., 1944.

Hayden, Robert C. *Seven Black American Scientists.* Reading, Massachusetts: Addison-Wesley Publishing Co., Inc., 1970.

Hillcourt, William. *Outdoor Things to Do: Year-Round Nature Fun for Girls and Boys.* New York: Golden Press, 1975.

Holt, Rackham. *George Washington Carver: An American Biography.* rev. ed. Garden City, New York: Doubleday & Co., Inc., 1963.

Hughes, Langston. *Famous American Negroes.* New York: Dodd, Mead & Co., 1954.

White, Anne Terry. *George Washington Carver: The Story of a Great American.* New York: Random House, 1953.

WALT DISNEY

"Disneyland really began when my two daughters were very young. Saturday was always Daddy's day, and I would take them to the merry-go-round and sit on a bench eating peanuts, while they rode. And sitting there alone, I felt that something should be built, some kind of family park where parents and children could have fun together."

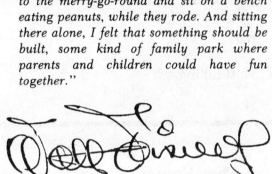

BIOGRAPHICAL SKETCH

Born in Chicago, Walter Elias Disney was one of five children raised in an atmosphere of hard work. The Disney family moved to a farm in Missouri, where Walt acquired his love for animals and made his first drawings. When he was six, Walt dipped a brush into a barrel of tar and decorated the white walls of the farmhouse with large drawings of animals. Afterward, his Aunt Maggie gave Walt a pad of drawing paper and a box of pencils in which he took an extraordinary interest. During the next years, Walt's interest in art continued to grow.

Walt was ambitious and while in his early twenties started work on a series of updated fairy tales. They were expertly made but did not sell. This forced Walt to close his studio. Undeterred, Walt took a train to Los Angeles, and in 1928 Mickey Mouse was created. Over the next few years, Walt produced *Steamboat Willie*, the first cartoon with synchronized sound, *Flowers and Trees*, the first full-color cartoon and *Snow White and the Seven Dwarfs*, the first full-length animated feature. In 1940, he produced *Fantasia*, a visual interpretation of orchestral music. Walt Disney's fame spread as he produced many more successful films, including *Mary Poppins*, *Davy Crockett*, *Dumbo* and *Bambi*.

Walt Disney's success involves a combination of hard work, practical knowledge, foresight, enterprise, and ingenuity. He formed the W.E.D (Walt Elias Disney) Enterprises, an "imagineering" team of experts in the fields of engineering, architecture, sculpture, and special effects. The purpose of W.E.D. Enterprises was to create a new kind of amusement park. Other amusement park owners ridiculed Disney's idea, believing that without the traditional attractions his venture would not succeed. Walt proved them wrong. Disneyland and Disney World are places where the young at heart of all ages can laugh, play and learn together.

CREATIVE ENCOUNTER #1.........A Class Discussion

"Of all the things I've done, the most vital is coordinating the talents of those who work for us and pointing them at a certain goal." W.E.D.

Walt Disney created a framework that supported the talents of many creative people.

Tending a garden, making a flower arrangement, or developing relationships with others are ways in which creativity is expressed. An individual can use his creative abilities in intellectual pursuits.

What were some of your first creations (finger painting, building a snowman)?

In what ways do you express your creative abilities now?

Make a class list of jobs/professions that require creative thinking.

CREATIVE ENCOUNTER #2.........Creative Questioning Techniques

Dr. E. Paul Torrance, educator and psychologist, has researched and written many books in the field of creativity. He reports that even after twenty minutes of explanation about the higher thinking processes grade school children showed an improvement in performing tasks of this type. In his research, Dr. Torrance noted the following four characteristics of creative thinking: fluency, flexibility, elaboration, and originality.

Fluency—producing many ideas

> The Carousel of Progress at Disney World traces 100 years of progress in America. Name many different conveniences made possible in American life by a century of innovation in electricity.

Flexibility—shifting one way of thinking (category) to another to produce a variety of ideas

> If Thomas Edison could visit Disney World, what do you think he would say?

> List objects that are shaped like circles. Each response should fall in a new category (ball, moon, pizza, dime). A response of penny, nickel, dime, quarter would not show flexible thinking.

Originality—producing clever or unique ideas

> Describe and illustrate your own ideas for a new attraction for Disneyland or Disney World.

> Draw a cartoon character that is different from those you are familiar with.

Elaboration—embellishing or expanding on an idea, adding detail

> Place your finger on an ink pad. Put your fingerprints on paper. Add details to your fingerprints to make an interesting picture.

"Like most people, I have fun just watching others have fun."
The right hemisphere of the brain is the area which controls abilities such as creativity, spatial thinking, imagination, and relationships. It also enables us to visualize.

Guided fantasy will help to develop this side of the brain to improve the skill called visual imagery. Close your eyes. As your teacher reads the imaginative journey, visualize yourself and others having fun at Disney World.

Pantomime scenes from your imaginative journey to Disney World.

Imaginative Journey to Disney World

Imagine the Florida sun shining brightly as you enter the Magic Kingdom at Disney World. You are warmly greeted by several Disney characters near a fragrant floral replica of Mickey Mouse. Welcome to this happy place.

You begin to walk down Main Street, U.S.A. Turn back the calender and recapture the flavor of a typical town of many years ago. Mickey Mouse leads you and your friends jubilantly down Main Street. Everyone in step, you all enjoy keeping cadence with the marching band as it plays "The Star-Spangled Banner."

You stop at Adventureland's Jungle Cruise and board a boat traveling down the mysterious rivers past a thundering waterfall to the exotic tropical regions of the world.

Back on land, you wander among the quaint shops of old New Orleans and view treasures from all over the world. Colorful flowers add beauty to the shops, streets and courtyards.

In the Hall of the Presidents you proudly watch the dramatic presentation of our nation's history as all the American Presidents come to life on stage. You listen to the inspiring words of Abraham Lincoln as he stately stands and speaks.

The melodious melody of "When You Wish Upon a Star" fills the air as you cross the moat and drawbridge of Sleeping Beauty's Castle. You enter the carefree kingdom of Fantasyland, where stories of childhood come to life. There's Donald Duck! Pluto, Goofy, Tigger, Pooh Bear and many other characters are also there to help you have a good time. There is music and dancing, and there you are twirling around with your favorite Disney friend. You are very busy posing for pictures and gathering autographs.

There's no time to rest and hardly time to catch your breath. "Fasten your seat belts," announces the automated voice over the loudspeaker. "You are about to experience a winding, soaring race through space on Space Mountain." Your heart beats a little faster as you secure your seatbelt. And then you are off speeding through the universe. After a safe reentry you tour Tomorrowland and view your world as it might well be.

As night falls, imagine a new kind of magic over Disney World. As you ride on the monorail and view the cascade of fireworks and dazzling lights of the Magic Kingdom, you are filled with wonderful memories. You store some of the wondrous visions in your mind, hoping they will last forever.

Your visit has been a fascinating journey to so many different worlds. You feel so close to Walt Disney and know that you too can create and envision everyday of your life . . . if you just take the time.

NAME _____

Try your hand at creative animation by creating your own original filmstrips. Below are three sets of filmstrips. Each strip contains six steps. In the first strip, the first and last steps are done for you, and you are to complete the steps in between. In the second strip, only the first step is done for you; you are to complete the remaining steps. The third strip is left to your creative imagination! Create anything you desire, but be sure to show something in a gradual state of change.

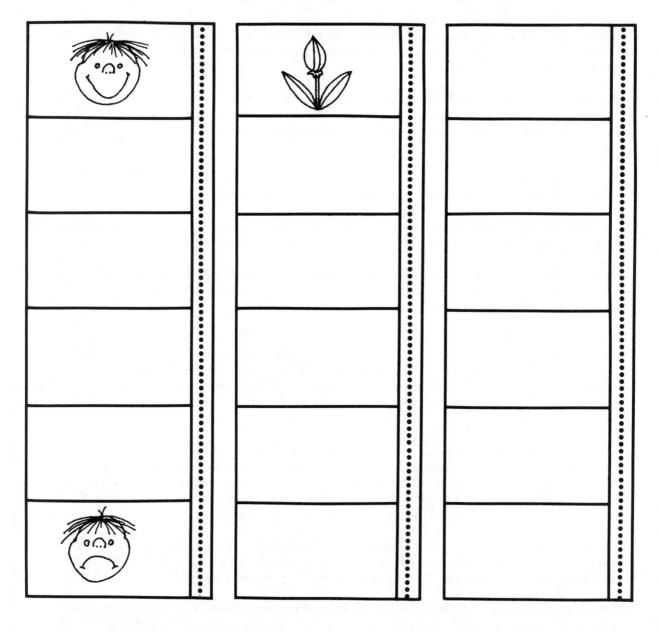

NAME _____

Solve the following picture puzzles. The arrangement of the letters, words, and/or numbers determines the meaning of the words or familiar phrases.

1.

2.

3.

mouse

Invent your own picture puzzles in the space below. ━━━━━━

41

INDEPENDENT PROJECTS—DISNEY

1. Make a collage. Use words and illustrations to express your visions and thoughts during your imaginative journey to Disney World.
2. Plan an imaginary trip to Disney World or Disneyland for you, your family or some friends. Use a map to calculate the number of miles you will travel. Organize a budget for your traveling expenses. Schedule the events for a three-day visit. Refer to *The Magic Kingdom of Disneyland and Walt Disney World.*
3. As you read *Chronicles of Narnia* by C.S. Lewis, try to improve your skill of visual imagery. Give a vivid and expressive presentation to your classmates about this series by using a variety of techniques: guided fantasy, an expressive voice, creative drama, colorful illustrations, a mural and props.
4. Use fingerprint designs and calligraphy to personalize your stationery or create your own greeting cards.
5. Create your own puppet show, play, game show or talk show. Use some of your classmates as participants or actors. Use music and sound effects in the background. Videotape your efforts.
6. Use *The Art of Walt Disney* and *Walt Disney's World of Fantasy* as references to research the basic techniques and elements of animated film and audio-animatronics. Be able to explain each technique and distinguish between them. Give examples.
7. Write a research paper about the prairie using *Walt Disney's Vanishing Prairie: A True Life Adventure* and *Walt Disney's People and Places* as references. What was the American prairie like?

RESOURCE BOOKS—DISNEY

Bailey, Adrian. *Walt Disney's World of Fantasy.* New York: Everest House Publishers, 1982.

Childs, Valerie. *The Magic of Disneyland and Walt Disney World.* New York: Mayflower Books, Inc., 1979.

Finch, Christopher. *The Art of Walt Disney: From Mickey Mouse to the Magic Kingdoms.* New York: Harry N. Abrams, Inc., 1975.

Geis, Darlene, ed. *Walt Disney's Treasury of Children's Classics.* New York: Harry N. Abrams, Inc., 1978.

Illustrated Disney Song Book. New York: Hal Leonard Publishing Corp., 1979.

Katz, Marjorie P. *Fingerprint Owls and Other Fantasies.* New York: M. Evans and Co., Inc., 1972.

Maltin, Leonard. *The Disney Films.* New York: Crown Publishers, Inc., 1973.

Montgomery, Elizabeth Rider. *Walt Disney: Master of Make-Believe.* Champaign, Illinois: Garrard Publishing Co., 1971.

Munsey, Cecil. *Disneyana: Walt Disney Collectibles.* New York: Hawthorn Books, Inc., 1974.

Watson, Jane Werner. *Walt Disney's People and Places.* New York: Golden Press, 1959.

Wayman, Joe. *The Other Side of Reading.* Carthage, Illinois: Good Apple, Inc., 1980.

Werner, Jane. *Walt Disney's Vanishing Prairie: A True Life Adventure.* New York: Simon and Schuster, Inc., 1955.

JAMES DOBSON

"By a proper use of parental influence and direction, we can provide our children with the inner strength necessary to survive the obstacles they will face. We can open the road to self-esteem and personal worth. Perhaps we won't reconstruct the world, but we can certainly help our children cope with it more successfully.

"I find it tremendously exciting to have an opportunity to express creativity in figuring out where people's needs are and where the hurts are and how to help them. I don't see myself as a crusader trying to change the world by myself, but I can do what I can. I can do my part.

"All I've attempted to do is to take the wisdom that's been with us for thousands of years and put it in a package that people find interesting and entertaining. Hopefully, it captures their imagination and provides the motivation to do what they probably already knew was right."

BIOGRAPHICAL SKETCH

Dr. James Dobson recalls that some of the happiest days of his life were when he was between ten and thirteen years of age. Dr. Dobson and his father would hike in a wooded area that he called the "big woods." They watched the breathtaking panorama of the morning unfold, the sunrise and the awakening of the animal world. During these times in the forest, they developed a closeness that made Jim want to be like his father.

James C. Dobson, Ph.D., is founder and president of Focus on the Family, a nonprofit organization dedicated to the preservation of the home. For fourteen years he was an Associate Clinical Professor of Pediatrics at the University of Southern California School of Medicine and served for seventeen years on the Attending Staff of Children's Hospital of Los Angeles in the Division of Child Development and Medical Genetics. He is a licensed psychologist in the state of California and the author of several best-selling books. He and his wife, Shirley, and their children, Danae and Ryan, reside in Southern California.

Dr. Dobson's first book for parents and teachers, *Dare to Discipline*, has now sold over one million copies and was selected in 1972 as one of fifty books to be rebound and placed in the White House Library. His subsequent eight books for the family are also best sellers.

Dr. Dobson is the host of his own radio program, heard nationwide on more than 500 stations. A film project consisting of seven films, seen by more than 40 million people, is also called *Focus on the Family*. Dr. Dobson has been a frequent guest on regional and national media programs. As a result of Dr. Dobson's radio and TV programs and films, he receives approximately 80,000 letters a month from individuals requesting family counsel and materials.

Dr. Dobson's influence has extended into the nation's Capital. He served as a Delegate at Large for the White House Conference on Families in 1980, and was subsequently appointed by President Carter to the Task Force which prepared the final White House Conference report. He has also been appointed by President Reagan to the National Advisory Committee for Juvenile Justice and Delinquency Prevention. In January, 1984, he was invited to the White House to consult with President Reagan on family matters.

CREATIVE ENCOUNTER #1.........Creative Drama

Dr. Dobson recalls the saddest day of his childhood in his book *Preparing for Adolescence.*

"Mother stopped the car immediately and ran back to where my dog lay. When he recognized her, Pippy wagged his stubby tail in appreciation. He was still wagging that little tail when his eyes grew glassy in death.

"Now it may not seem so terrible to lose a dog, but Pippy's death was like the end of the world for me. I simply cannot describe how important he was to me when I was thirteen years old. He was my very special friend whom I loved more than anyone can imagine. I could talk to him about things that no one else seemed to understand. He was always in a good mood, even when I was not. ...And my father, who had told me to take the loss like a man, bawled like a baby on that day behind the grapevine."

Role play the following situation: Your friend received a warm, cuddly puppy for a surprise birthday gift. Every day Fluffy excitedly welcomed your friend home from school. One day his loyal companion was not there. Your friend is very sad about the death of his pet and comes to you for help. How will you comfort your friend?

CREATIVE ENCOUNTER #2.........A Class Discussion

"My own dad decided when I was eight years old that he was going to teach me to play tennis. I was not at all enthusiastic about this offer, because it meant hard work. But Dad wanted me to play tennis, and I respected him too much to turn him down. So we spent several agonizing Saturdays on the court. He would hit me a ball and I'd whack it over the fence, and then have to go get it. I couldn't have been less motivated, but I tried to act involved. 'You think I'm getting it, Dad?' I said, as another ball flew straight up.

"About a month later, however, things began to click. I slowly began to realize what this game had to offer me. The spark of enthusiasm turned into a flame that still burns. All through high school and college it was my source of self-confidence. If asked to write, 'Who am I?' during the trials of adolescence, I would have begun, 'I am the number-one tennis player in the high school.' If my dad had not planted his thumb in my back, urging me to try something new, I'd have never known what I missed. I am thankful that he helped me compensate."

Describe an experience when you were reluctant to try a new task, sport, or skill. Who encouraged you to try something new?

Share how your practice, hard work, and achievement helped to build your self-confidence.

Discuss and evaluate your skills in task commitment.

How much encouragement or reward do you need to become involved in a task? (This type of motivation is called extrinsic motivation. Intrinsic motivation involves a deep desire to carry on a certain kind of activity for the joy it brings.)

Do you bring enthusiasm and determination to your work?

What is your incentive for completing your tasks?

Are you willing to do your chores for the personal satisfaction of completing a task or is your allowance your only incentive?

What can you do to consistently improve and complete your tasks?

CREATIVE ENCOUNTER #3..........Building Self-Confidence

In *Hide or Seek* Dr. Dobson states that inferiority, the depressing feeling of worthlessness, can either crush and paralyze an individual or it can provide tremendous emotional energy which powers every kind of success or achievement. The following are his suggestions for climbing out of the canyon of inferiority: Remember that you are not alone. Face your problems. Compensate or make up for your weaknesses by developing your strengths. Work to develop genuine friends.

1. Look up the word *empathy* in the dictionary. Write the definition.

   _____

   _____

   _____

2. A person says to you, *"I am dealing with my own inadequacies pretty well and now feel I am ready to take additional steps in the direction of self-confidence. What do you recommend?"*

   Try to empathize with that person and write down what advice you would give to him/her.

   _____

   _____

   _____

   _____

Discuss your answer with your classmates.

Here is part of Dr. Dobson's answer to this letter.

"I have repeatedly observed that a person's own needs and problems seem less threatening when he is busy helping someone else handle theirs! It is difficult to concentrate on your own troubles when you are actively shouldering another person's load and seeking solutions to his problems. Therefore, I would recommend that you consciously make a practice of giving to others. Visit the sick. Bake something for your neighbors. And perhaps most important, learn to be a good listener. The world is filled with lonely, disheartened people like you were, and you are in an excellent position to empathize with them. And while you're doing it, I guarantee that your own sense of uselessness will begin to fade."

CREATIVE ENCOUNTER #4..........Accepting Others

In *Preparing for Adolescence* Dr. Dobson shares an experience when he was nine years old.

"I told everyone that Fred had 'Jeep-fender ears,' because of their curved shapes, and my friends thought that was terribly funny. They all laughed and began calling him 'Jeep Fenders.' Fred seemed to be accepting the joke pretty well. He sat with a little smile on his face (because he didn't know what to say), but it was hurting him deeply. Suddenly Fred stopped smiling. He exploded from his chair and hurried toward the door, crying.

"I didn't realize I was hurting his feelings. No one had shown me that others were as sensitive to being laughed at as I was. That's why I want to be sure that you will know what I didn't know.

"If a person is too tall or short or fat or thin, don't make fun of him, don't give him a nickname, don't call attention to the feature he's already sensitive about, and don't give him any other reasons to feel bad. He has enough problems already."

1. How do you feel when someone laughs at you?

_____

_____

_____

_____

2. What advice would you give a person who has been teased in a cruel way?

_____

_____

_____

_____

3. Draw a cartoon that illustrates how one might deal with peer pressure or pressure to conform.

CREATIVE ENCOUNTER #5.........Making Friends

Dr. Dobson states that true friends will help your self-concept, the way you feel about yourself.

1. What are qualities of a friend?

_____

_____

_____

_____

_____

2. *"I have a very hard time making friends. Can you help me learn how to influence people and make them like me?"*
   Write some helpful advice for this person.

_____

_____

_____

_____

_____

Discuss your answer with your classmates.

Here is Dr. Dobson's answer to this letter. Discuss the answer.

" 'The best way to have a friend is to be a good friend to others.' That's a very old proverb, but it's still true. Now let me give you a little clue that will help you deal with people of any age. Most people experience feelings of inferiority and self-doubt, as I have described. And if you understand and remember that fact, it will help you know the secret of social success. Never make fun of others or ridicule them. Let them know that you respect and accept them, and that they are important to you. Make a conscious effort to be sensitive to their feelings, and protect their reputations. I think you'll quickly find that many will do the same for you in return."

CREATIVE ENCOUNTER #6..........Family Traditions

Dr. Dobson gives the following advice for coping with dangers of overcommitment and stress in *Dr. Dobson Answers Your Questions:*

"I emphasize the importance of creating special traditions in your home. By tradition I'm referring to those recurring events and behaviors that are anticipated, especially by children, as times of closeness and fellowship between loved ones. The great value of traditions is that they give a family a sense of identity and belonging."

Write a composition about your family traditions.

Tell about your family gatherings on holidays and what your family enjoys eating and doing together.

_____

_____

_____

_____

_____

_____

_____

_____

_____

_____

_____

Write the names of your family in this family tree.

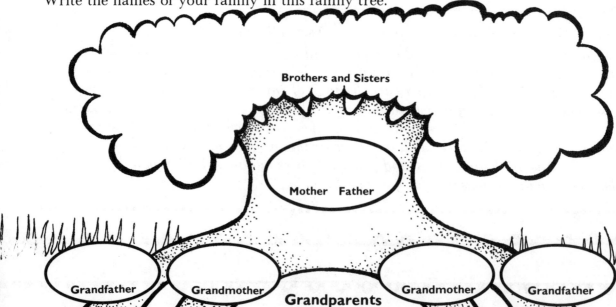

Brothers and Sisters

Mother   Father

Grandfather   Grandmother   **Grandparents**   Grandmother   Grandfather

CREATIVE ENCOUNTER #7.........Designing a Flag

In *Hide or Seek* Dr. Dobson suggests this activity to help build self-esteem.

"That flag is then flown in the front yard on the child's 'special' days, including birthdays, after he has received an A in school, when he scores a goal in soccer, or hits a home run in baseball, and so forth."

Design your own flag, which can then be sewn on canvas or cloth.

INDEPENDENT PROJECTS—DOBSON

1. Write about what your family means to you.
2. Make a scrapbook of your family traditions and American traditions. Include photographs, your autobiography, and your composition about family gatherings and family activities.
3. Set up a counseling service. Make a mailbox for your friends in which to place their letters, stating their problems and questions. With your teacher's guidance answer their letters with advice.
4. Plan a fireside chat, which is a time when a few students can informally get together to talk about their problems and interests.
5. Design certificates of achievement for your teachers, classmates, and family.
6. Plan a Secret Pal Week. Exchange names and surprise your secret pal with notes of encouragement, sincere compliments, and gifts.
7. Plan a Grandparents' Day. Honor your grandparents and ask them to tell stories about their lives.
8. Research a topic in psychology, such as counseling or listening techniques.
9. Plan a debate and state your opinions about the effects of television in the home.
10. Make posters about the dangers of drugs, drinking and smoking.
11. What are some of our American traditions? Write about the development of some of them.
12. Research the early American holidays, such as the first Thanksgiving and the first July 4th celebration.

RESOURCE BOOKS—DOBSON

Dobson, James. *Dare to Discipline*. Wheaton, Illinois: Tyndale House Publishers, Inc., 1970.

Dobson, James. *Dr. Dobson Answers Your Questions*. Wheaton, Illinois: Tyndale House Publishers, Inc., 1982.

Dobson, James. *Hide or Seek: How to Build Self-Esteem in Your Child*. rev. ed. Old Tappan, New Jersey: Fleming H. Revell Co., 1979.

Dobson, James. *Preparing for Adolescence*. Santa Ana, California: Vision House Publishers, 1978.

Dobson, James. *Preparing for Adolescence Growthguide: A Manual to Accompany Preparing for Adolescence*. Santa Ana, California: Vision House Publishers, 1979.

Dobson, James. *The Strong-Willed Child: Birth Through Adolescence*. Wheaton, Illinois: Tyndale House Publishers, Inc., 1978.

Dobson, Shirley, and Gloria Gaither. *Let's Make a Memory*. Waco, Texas: Word Books, 1983.

THOMAS EDISON

"We can derive the most satisfying kind of joy from thinking and thinking and thinking. Imagination supplies the ideas. Technical knowledge carries them out. The three great essentials to achieve anything worthwhile are first hard work; second, stick-to-itiveness; third, common sense.

"My desire is to do everything within my power to free the people from drudgery, and create the largest measure of happiness and prosperity. If our work has widened the horizon of man's understanding and given even a little measure of happiness in this world, I am content."

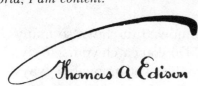

BIOGRAPHICAL SKETCH

Thomas Alva Edison had an investigative and observing mind, and he persistently asked many questions. Before he knew his ABC's, he was found copying store signs on his slate. Among his early experiments were sitting on a nest of goose eggs for hours, trying to make his friend fly, and building a fire in a barn. Three months of school was all the formal education he received. After his teachers reported him as "addled," his mother taught him at home and gave him a love for learning. When he was ten years old, he read college-level books and set up a laboratory in the cellar.

At the age of twelve, he sold newspapers and before he was fifteen, he became a publisher with his printing press on a train. A trainman caught hold of his ears to pull him up to the platform of a moving train, and this caused him to grow deaf. He established a "laboratory on wheels," but a stick of phosphorus ignited and set the baggage car on fire. At the age of fifteen, he saved the life of a child who had been playing on a railroad track. In gratitude, the child's father taught Thomas Edison telegraphy.

Thomas Alva Edison laughed, whistled, and sang at work. Sometimes he would sleep on a desk in his laboratory with a stack of books for a pillow. He proposed to his bride-to-be, by tapping his message of love in the Morse code.

Curiosity, patience, perseverance, and hard work helped make his dreams come true. Instead of worrying about what had happened, he was interested in making something happen. He explained, *"I have no interest in spilt milk."*

Thomas Edison is credited with more than 1,000 inventions and improvements, including the phonograph, moving pictures, the dictaphone, and a duplicating machine. However, his major contribution to the world consists of his invention of the electric light and in making it available to the world by designing one of the world's first electric-power stations. When he was honored by other governments, he said the honor was not for him but for his country. The inscription on the Congressional Medal of Honor stated, *"He illuminated the path of progress by his inventions."*

CREATIVE ENCOUNTER #1..........Learning Perseverance

"In trying to perfect a thing, I sometimes run straight up against a granite wall a hundred feet high. The incandescent light was the hardest one of all; it took many years not only of concentrated thought but also of worldwide research."

Thomas Edison had to overcome insurmountable obstacles to achieve success. After his team of workers suffered from heartbreaking failures, Thomas Edison would often encourage them by starting the next morning on similar trials with new hope, joy, and enthusiasm.

What have you accomplished that required perseverance? Share experiences about failures or setbacks that were stepping-stones to success. How can we cope with failure and success?

CREATIVE ENCOUNTER #2..........A Class Discussion

"Suppose . . . we show to the child . . . the cocoon unfolding, the butterfly actually emerging. The knowledge which comes from the actual seeing is worthwhile."

If you had one hour of free time, what would you do? Thomas Edison could not imagine being bored, for he liked to work, experiment, and think. He was keenly aware of little things and searched for new ideas.

People can face a task with different reactions. "Oh, I have mowed the lawn so many times. It's boring." "Oh, it's a beautiful day to work outside." Do you catch yourself saying, "I'm bored"? Do you use your imagination and ability to discover innovative ways to challenge yourself?

Thomas Edison believed that people should start as early as possible to observe, study, and think to discover ideas and draw conclusions about the world and nature. What goals will you set to stop thoughts of boredom and build new thinking habits of challenge?

Here are examples: Next time you are waiting in line, keep your mind busy. Make up new brain teasers.

While taking a long journey in a car, make up a creative story about the trees and scenery.

When you have free time, write a letter to a friend, offer to help someone, conduct a nature study and hike, or play chess.

On his seventy-fifth birthday, Thomas Edison stated that he had enough inventions to keep him busy for another hundred years. When you catch yourself thinking that you are in an incredibly dull situation, change your thinking patterns. Develop your thinking skills. Try to remove the word *boring* from your vocabulary. Replace these thoughts of boredom with thoughts and ideas that challenge. Challenge yourself to discover new horizons! Cultivate the gift of wonder!

CREATIVE ENCOUNTER #3..........A Panel Discussion

Research the lives of the Wright Brothers, Cyrus McCormick, Benjamin Franklin, Johann Gutenberg, and other inventors.

Represent the life of one of these inventors. Speak and act as if you were this inventor in a panel discussion with your friends, who act as other inventors. Contrast life before and after their inventions.

CREATIVE ENCOUNTER #4..........Our American Heritage

"My message to you is to be courageous. I have lived a long time. I have seen history repeat itself again and again. I have seen many 'depressions' in business. Always America has come out strong and more prosperous. Be as brave as your fathers were before you. Have faith—go forward."

Read about the lives of George Washington, Abraham Lincoln, and Abigail Adams. Study the Constitution and Declaration of Independence. What goals did early Americans have for the United States? Give a speech about our American heritage and the dreams, goals, struggles, and accomplishments of early Americans.

CREATIVE ENCOUNTER #5..........Newspaper Projects

Write a news article from the point of view of a reporter interviewing Clara Barton, Thomas Jefferson, Florence Nightingale or another historical figure.

Bring newspapers and other references to class and lead a discussion about current events. Write a news story as it might have appeared in the newspaper on July 4, 1776, and another as it might appear on July 4, 2076.

CREATIVE ENCOUNTER #6..........Appreciating People

"I discovered in early life what a good thing a mother was. When she came out as my strong defender, when the school teacher called me 'addled,' I determined then that I would be worthy of her and show her that her confidence was not misplaced. She was so true, so sure of me. I felt that I had someone to live for, someone I must not disappoint. She was always kind and sympathetic and never seemed to misunderstand or misjudge me.

"The good effects of her early training I can never lose. If it had not been for her appreciation and her faith in me at a critical time in my experience, I should very likely never have become an inventor. You see, she believed that many of the boys who turned out badly by the time they grew to manhood would have become valuable citizens if they had been handled in the right way when they were young. Her years of experience as a school teacher taught her many things about human nature and especially about boys. I was always a careless boy, and with a mother of a different character I should have probably turned out badly. But her firmness, her sweetness, her goodness, were potent powers to keep me in the right path. The memory of her will always be a blessing to me."

If you could give any gift in the world to a special person in your life, what would it be?

Think of the special people who have inspired you. Remember, also, that you can help others to achieve greatness by encouraging them to believe in themselves. Express your thoughts in creative writing about special people in your life who believe in you and share your hopes and dreams. Also, share how you have influenced others and how you plan to continue to help others. Write notes of appreciation to your special people, and let them know you care.

CREATIVE ENCOUNTER #7..........Special People

Discover more about special people with the following activity. Find a person in the room who fits one of the descriptions. Place his or her name in the appropriate space provided. Continue until all blanks are filled.

Fill in each blank with a person's name.

_____ has read a book for fun in the last week.

_____ plays a musical instrument.

_____ has planned and carried out an experiment.

_____ makes up brain teasers, puzzles, or riddles.

_____ has been camping recently.

_____ likes to go horseback riding.

_____ has a close friend from another state.

_____ has baked cookies.

_____ has an unusual pet.

_____ likes to travel.

_____ has sung a solo.

_____ has worked in a garden.

_____ has a pen pal from another state or country.

_____ has been to a museum.

_____ has an extraordinary hobby or pastime.

_____ has an idea for an invention.

_____ has visited a foreign country.

_____ learned a new skill recently.

_____ likes to read about American history.

_____ plans to attend college.

_____ is active in 4-H (or other clubs).

_____ likes sports.

_____ likes to draw or paint.

_____ has the same number of brothers and sisters as you.

_____ celebrates his birthday in the same month as yours.

CREATIVE ENCOUNTER #8..........Uninvented Inventions

"When I want to discover something, I begin by reading up everything that has been done along that line in the past—that's what all these books in the library are for. I see what has been accomplished at great labor and expense in the past. I gather the data of many thousands of experiments as a starting point, and then I make thousands more."

1. Brainstorm: Name some uninvented inventions. _____

_____

_____

_____

_____

_____

2. What would you like to invent to make life better? _____

_____

_____

_____

_____

_____

3. Draw and design your uninvented invention. _____

Plan and present an advertisement of your uninvented invention.

INDEPENDENT PROJECTS—EDISON

1. Continue an indepth study of the characteristics and life of Thomas Edison.
2. Contrast life before and after the inventions of Thomas Edison.
3. Evaluate how people meet failure and success. List ways to cope with failure and success.
4. Diagram a chart of inventions in historical sequence.
5. Examine and sketch the inventions of Thomas Edison and other inventors.
6. Experiment, design, and build your own inventions.
7. Build a telegraph and learn the Morse code.
8. Learn how to operate computers.
9. Make a scrapbook of inventions and events that have occurred in your lifetime.
10. Summarize a newspaper article into a short telegram or bumper sticker.
11. Create a skit or play about Thomas Edison and other American inventors and pioneers.

RESOURCE BOOKS—EDISON

Cousins, Margaret. *The Story of Thomas Alva Edison.* New York: Random House, 1965.

Eberle, Irmengarde. *Famous Inventors for Young People.* New York: Dodd, Mead & Co., Inc., 1941.

Ellis, Keith. *Thomas Edison: Genius of Electricity.* New York: Crane, Russak & Co., Inc., 1974.

Hiebert, Roselyn, and Ray Eldon. *Thomas Edison: American Inventor.* New York: Franklin Watts, Inc., 1969.

Hutchings, David W. *Edison at Work: The Thomas A. Edison Laboratory at West Orange, New Jersey.* New York: Hastings House, Publishers, 1969.

Meadowcroft, William H. *The Boy's Life of Edison.* New York: Harper & Brothers, Publishers, 1921.

Meyer, Jerome S. *World Book of Great Inventions.* New York: The World Publishing Co., 1956.

Neal, Harry Edward. *From Spinning Wheel to Spacecraft: The Story of the Industrial Revolution.* New York: Julian Messner, Inc., 1964.

North, Sterling. *Young Thomas Edison.* Boston: Houghton Mifflin Co., 1958.

Pratt, Fletcher. *All About Famous Inventors and Their Inventions.* New York: Random House, 1955.

Tunis, Edwin. *The Young United States, 1789-1830.* New York: The World Publishing Co., 1969.

Weiss, Harvey. *How to Be an Inventor.* New York: Thomas Y. Crowell, 1980.

HENRY FORD

"There was too much hard hand labour on our own and all other farms of the time. Even when very young I suspected that much might somehow be done in a better way. That is what took me into mechanics—although my mother always said that I was born a mechanic. I had a kind of workshop with odds and ends of metal for tools before I had anything else. In those days we did not have the toys of today; what we had were home-made. My toys were all tools—they still are! And every fragment of machinery was a treasure.

"I deeply admire the men who founded this country, and I think we ought to know more about them and how they lived and the force and courage they had. Of course we can read about them but . . . the only way to show how our forefathers lived and to bring to mind what kind of people they were is to reconstruct, as near-ly as possible, the exact conditions under which they lived."

Henry Ford

BIOGRAPHICAL SKETCH

From childhood Henry had a mechanical curiosity and aptitude. At the age of twelve Henry was driving a wagon with his father when they met a steam engine, the first vehicle not drawn by horses that Henry had seen. From that time on, his great interest was in making a machine that would travel the roads.

Henry developed early into a leader, and other boys followed him in his schemes and experiments. During noon recess they built a dam on a creek that ran near the school. That night a heavy rain caused the stream to overflow into a neighboring farmer's potato patch. The next day the young engineers were ordered to tear out the dam. On another occasion they constructed a steam tur-bine, which suddenly exploded and set the school fence on fire.

Henry liked to explore anything mechanical. When a new toy came into the Ford home, someone would exclaim, *"Don't let Henry see it! He'll take it apart."* On his thirteenth birthday he received a watch; he promptly took it apart and put it back together again. Henry's father wanted him to continue to work on the farm but did not stand in the way of Henry's desire to learn more about machinery.

At the age of sixteen Henry left the farm with less than five dollars in his pocket and walked to Detroit. During the 1880's he had several jobs, where he learned more about machinery. Henry Ford was highly regarded at the Edison Illuminating Company and was promoted to chief engineer in 1893. At a company banquet Thomas Edison was enthusiastic and said, *"Young man, that's the thing! You have it—the self-contained unit carrying its own fuel with it! Keep at it!"* En-couragement from this inventor filled Henry Ford with new inspiration.

Henry was making good progress in his workshop, a little brick shed behind his home. Finally, at two o'clock on the rainy morning of June 4, 1896, Henry's horseless carriage was finished. While others scoffed, Henry Ford pursued his goals with initiative and hard work. He organized the Ford Motor Company in 1903. By the year of the Model T in 1908 the automobile industry was boom-ing.

Henry Ford became a symbol of American industrial ingenuity. His successful demonstration of the assembly line method and mass production revolutionized transportation, industry, and economics throughout the world.

CREATIVE ENCOUNTER #1.........Creative Drama

"If I stopped my machine anywhere, a crowd was around it before I could start it up again. If I left it alone for even a minute some inquisitive person always tried to run it. Finally, I had to carry a chain and chain it to a lamppost whenever I left it anywhere."

Imagine what life was like before the invention of the horseless carriage. What do you think were the reactions of the people who saw the horseless carriage for the first time?

Dramatize these reactions.

CREATIVE ENCOUNTER #2..........A Class Discussion

"I will build a motor car for the great multitude. It will be large enough for the family but small enough for the individual to run and care for. It will be constructed of the best materials, by the best men to be hired, after the simplest design that modern engineering can devise. But it will be so low in price that no man making a good salary will be unable to own one—and enjoy with his family the blessing of hours of pleasure in God's great open spaces."

Contrast life in America before and after the invention of the automobile.

Brainstorm: List all the uses you can think of for old automobile tires.

Identify all the automobiles you can think of, such as the school bus, fire engine, and grain truck, that are important to various jobs.

If you were an automobile manufacturer and wanted to make your automobile look different from the others, what parts would you change? What are the problems of the automobile today? What ways would you suggest to solve these problems? What safety features and convenience features would you suggest?

CREATIVE ENCOUNTER #3..........Automobile of the Future

"But if one has visions of service, if one has vast plans which no ordinary resources could possibly realize, if one has a life ambition to make the industrial desert bloom like the rose, and the work-a-day life suddenly blossom into fresh and enthusiastic human motives of higher character and efficiency, then one sees in large sums of money what the farmer sees in his seed corn—the beginning of new and richer harvests whose benefits can no more be selfishly confined than can the sun's rays."

Imagine yourself driving the automobile of the future. What is it like? In what ways do you think automobiles of the future will be different from the automobiles of today? How will the automobile run in the future? How fast do you predict it will drive?

Design an automobile of the future on paper.

Display the drawing in your classroom.

Create an advertisement about this future automobile.

While the introduction is read, close your eyes and think about being an automobile. Become an automobile in your imagination. Respond to the questions as though you are an automobile.

Imagine snow-peaked mountains touching the clouds in the distance, sunshine reflecting on a crystal-clear lake, wild flowers swaying in the breeze, and a fawn curiously peeking around a tree in the forest. You are to become an automobile traveling on the curvy road which winds around the mountain.

1. What kind of automobile are you?
2. What color are you?
3. How fast are you traveling?
4. What is your destination?
5. You just passed someone who took a second look at you. What do you consider your most outstanding feature?
6. You just stopped for a train at a railroad crossing. You heard a plane roaring above and saw a sailboat serenely sailing on the lake. What do you think are the most interesting features about the other forms of transportation?
7. Skidding to a sudden halt to avoid a collision, you just missed plunging off a steep cliff. How do you feel, and what did you almost hit?
8. A truck driver has just asked your driver to drag race on the winding road to see who reaches the top of the mountain first. Your driver agrees. How do you feel about this?
9. It just rained, but now it is colder and it has started to snow. Now it is time for the long journey down the mountain. What will this do to you as you travel down the mountain, and how do you feel about it?
10. If you could change anything about the transportation system of the automobile, what would you change?

INDEPENDENT PROJECTS—FORD

1. Henry Ford once wrote in a diary, *"Could read all the first readers before I started school. My mother taught me."* Locate and read excerpts from the *McGuffey Readers*. Give an oral interpretation of an excerpt from the *McGuffey Readers* to your class.
2. Later in his life Henry Ford stated that the *McGuffey Readers* greatly influenced his life. What are your favorite books? Make a list of these books. Choose three of the books and explain how they have influenced your life.
3. *"Mass production is the focusing upon a manufacturing project of the principles of power, accuracy, economy, system, continuity, speed, and repetition."* Research the jobs and products that are involved in the designing and manufacturing of the automobile.
4. Plan and draw a map of an imaginary trip via your automobile. Write about your trip from the viewpoint of your automobile.
5. Prepare a class lesson and illustrations about your research of the various kinds of automobiles of the past, present, and future.
6. Explain in a news broadcast about unique automobiles around the world.
7. Diagram a chart about the parts of the engine and the automobile.
8. Make and display your chart of safety rules.
9. Explain the steps of changing a tire or checking the oil.
10. Research the advantages and disadvantages of the steam engine, diesel engine, gasoline engine, and electric motor.

RESOURCE BOOKS—FORD

Barry, James P. *Henry Ford and Mass Production: An Inventor Builds a Car that Millions Can Afford.* New York: Franklin Watts, Inc., 1973.

Bendick, Jeanne. *The First Book of Automobiles.* rev. ed. New York: Franklin Watts, Inc., 1978.

Bolton, Sarah K. *Lives of Poor Boys Who Became Famous.* New York: Thomas Y. Crowell Co., 1962.

Caldwell, Cy. *Henry Ford.* New York: Julian Messner, Inc., 1947.

Clymer, Floyd. *Henry's Wonderful Model T, 1908-1927.* New York: Bonanza Books, 1955.

Ford, Henry. *My Life and Work.* Garden City, New York: Garden City Publishing Co., 1926.

Harding, Anthony, ed. *Car: Facts and Feats.* New York: Sterling Publishing Co., Inc., 1977.

Kelly, Regina Z. *Henry Ford.* Chicago: Follett Publishing Co., 1970.

Lindberg, Stanley W. *The Annotated McGuffey: Selections from the McGuffey Eclectic Readers 1836-1920.* New York: Van Nostrand Reinhold Co., 1976.

Olson, Sidney. *Young Henry Ford: A Picture History of the First Forty Years.* Detroit: Wayne State University, 1963.

Richards, Kenneth. *People of Destiny: Henry Ford.* Chicago: Children's Press, Inc., 1967.

Waitley, Douglas. *The Roads We Traveled: An Amusing History of the Automobile.* New York: Julian Messner, Inc., 1979.

GENE GETZ

"*I had the privilege of being the firstborn child of wonderful parents. We had the usual problems of growing up, of course. But we were basically a close-knit family. Sure, as kids we had our knock-down drag-outs, and we all went through the usual selfish stages that all kids go through. But I distinctly remember, as the oldest, that 'fighting with each other' was **our** privilege—no one else's. Let no one else lay a hand on my brothers and sisters! I was ready to defend them.*

"*And Mom and Dad? They made mistakes; they were far from perfect. But they were **our** parents. They loved us and cared for us. They were devoted to us even when we were anything but appreciative and cooperative. And their greatest contribution to us was our spiritual heritage—the knowledge that we could become a part of the family of God.*"

Gene A. Getz

BIOGRAPHICAL SKETCH

Gene Getz, his three brothers and three sisters, one of whom died at age three, grew up on a farm in Medaryville, Indiana. As an energetic child, Gene took care of his horse named Marvel and helped with the chores on the farm. Today the Getz siblings enjoy getting together to reminisce and reflect on their childhood experiences.

Dr. Gene A. Getz is a graduate of Moody Bible Institute in Chicago and Rocky Mountain College in Billings, Montana. He received his M.A. degree from Wheaton Graduate School in Wheaton, Illinois, and his Ph.D. from New York University. At the age of twenty-three, Dr. Getz was asked to teach at the college level. He taught at Moody Bible Institute for thirteen years and then served for six years as a full-time professor at Dallas Theological Seminary. Dr. Getz currently teaches part time at Dallas Seminary and serves as Senior Pastor at Fellowship Bible Church North in Plano, Texas, a growing Dallas suburb. He also directs the Center for Church Renewal, an organization designed to serve pastors, missionaries, and other church leaders.

Dr. Getz has written almost twenty-five books, which focus on the importance of the family, guidelines for living, and building relationships with people. Some of his best-selling books are *The Measure of a Man*, *The Measure of a Family*, and *The Measure of a Woman*. Frequent speaking engagements, lectures at seminars, presentations of his video cassette series, and the involvement of thousands have resulted in the spread of his beliefs and philosophies across the nation. Audience participation followed by group discussion is the hallmark of a Gene Getz presentation.

Dr. Getz resides in Dallas, Texas, with his wife Elaine and their children, Renee, Kenton, and Robyn and her husband, Bob. The Getz family enjoys snow skiing, racquetball, watching the Dallas Cowboys, and riding motorcycles in the mountains.

CREATIVE ENCOUNTER #1.........A Class Discussion

*"I remember a specific incident that happened when I was in first grade. The teacher, Olive Owens, had outlined the word **me** in a beautiful cursive style on the chalkboard. She then told us to copy the word on our papers.*

*"I had never written a single **letter** in my life, let alone a **word**. Those were pre-Sesame Street days! Try as I might, I couldn't get my pencil to cooperate.*

"To my dismay, Miss Owens began to look at each student's work—one by one. I was in the third row of seats. She completed row one, came up row two, and then started down row three. My heart was pounding. What would she think of my inability? What would she do? These were pressing questions in my six-year-old heart.

"And there she was, looking straight down at my paper and a few marks that resembled more a runaway seismograph than the efforts of a six-year-old boy. My heart was pounding even more and I was so overwhelmed with fear that I broke into tears.

"At that moment, Miss Owens did something I'll never forget. She leaned over, and with a compassionate voice said, 'That's alright, Gene.' Then she sealed her words with a gentle kiss on my cheek.

"To this day I remember that wonderful moment. It dispelled my fears and gave me courage to try again. I'm convinced that my teacher's gentle words helped me to take a giant step in the direction of liking school, rather than hating it.

"The quality of gentleness is powerful in dealing with people of all ages. It can soften the heart of a child as well as an adult. It can create beautiful memories and it can dissipate anger."

Think of a situation in your own life when a person's kindness and encouragement influenced you. Describe this situation to the class. What would have happened if that person had responded to you with criticism rather than kindness? How do you react when you are criticized for something you've tried but failed? How do you feel when you are praised for your effort and encouraged to try again?

CREATIVE ENCOUNTER #2.........Learning to Encourage

"One day a friend and I were riding our motorcycles in the mountains. We were following a winding dirt trail, and suddenly we looked out ahead. There rising majestically into the sky was one of the most beautiful Spanish peaks in southern Colorado. We pulled our motorcycles to a stop and drank in the beauty.

"Then I noticed what made the mountain so captivating. It was naturally framed by a long hanging branch above us. To our left was a sloping cliff that formed the frame on that side. Rising up from the mountainside were some gorgeous trees on the right. To 'top it off' the clouds above the mountain were hovering at just the right angle. Actually, that beautiful Spanish peak looked just like 'apples of gold in settings of silver.'

"Words spoken in the right circumstances at the right time are just as captivating and memorable as that mountain. I'll never forget that scene as long as I live. I can remember words that are just as vivid. I'm sure you can too.

"Are you using your potential to encourage others? You should. It is a skill that every one of us can develop. In fact, it usually doesn't come naturally. It takes practice."

Brainstorm: Think of phrases that express encouragement and words of praise. Make stickers, certificates, or bookmarks with these phrases. Give them to the special people in your life. Here are examples: Thanks for being you. I'm proud of you. Very creative. Good thinking. That's a good observation. I appreciate your work. Thank you for your understanding. That was very kind of you.

CREATIVE ENCOUNTER #3.........Improving Performance

"When I entered college as a student I took their entrance exam in composition. Believe it or not, I flunked! I didn't know the difference between 'was' and 'were' in the English language. I was always used to saying 'we done it' rather than 'we did it!' Can you believe that I was asked to simply write a paragraph on why I came to this particular college. I think I got about three lines on this page and was stymied.

"The point, of course, is that this became an incredible challenge to me. I dug into the remedial composition course with great fervor, not realizing that eventually I would end up writing about 25 books."

Identify an area (a subject in school, a sport, etc.) in which you're having a difficult time. Try to analyze why this area is so hard for you. Think of ways in which you could improve your performance. For example, perhaps you could spend extra time per day working on this area or get special tutoring. Write up a plan of action for improving your performance. After a designated time period, report on the results of your plan.

CREATIVE ENCOUNTER #4.........Creative Drama

"Learning to control what we say in some respects is like learning to ski, which is one of my favorite sports. Beginners always stumble and fall. There is no other way to learn.

"But as you're learning, you discover how to control yourself. You learn to control the mountain rather than allowing the mountain to control you. But with each step of progress, you tend to regress—often to a prone position—until you have mastered the next level of difficulty. In fact, I've often said that if you're not falling you're not progressing.

"Finally, you become an advanced skier. But lo and behold, you find there is always more to learn. And even when you feel you're in total control, if you're not careful you'll suddenly find yourself flat on your face or your back—depending on what happens at the moment.

"No matter how good you are, you can make mistakes. Usually it happens when you're not concentrating; perhaps when you're tired; mostly when you're overconfident; and quite frequently when you're 'showing off.' And you always fall when you're over your head, when you're trying new approaches, when you're stretching yourself. And it usually happens when you least expect it.

"And so it is with learning to control what we say. Learning to live is a process. And we never arrive. We're never perfect. Mature? Yes! But never exempt from failure along the way."

Pantomime the following scene: You desperately want to learn to ski. You have signed up for lessons. You try and try, but you just can't seem to catch on. After falling time after time, you're ready to give up and admit defeat, but suddenly something clicks! You find yourself sailing down the slope with a feeling of exhilaration and a sense of pride. You did it! You didn't quit! You learned to ski—maybe not perfectly, but you're on your way!

"Having been reared on a farm in Indiana, I remember the times when we planted corn and then waited for rain. There were times when it didn't come and the seed lay in the ground, unable to germinate because of the lack of moisture. There were also times that there was enough moisture to cause the seed to sprout and begin to grow, but lack of rain caused the plants to stop growing. Leaves turned yellow then brown. And I remember times that there was not enough moisture for the ears of corn to develop on the stalks.

"Those days of waiting were trying and difficult for my father, because a bad crop would mean a poor harvest. And a poor harvest meant little or no income for that year. And all of us can identify to some degree with what it would mean to lose a year's income, especially when you've used all your reserves to prepare the soil, buy the seed and fertilizer, and to go to the expense of planting the fields."

Describe a situation in your life when you had to wait for something. How did you feel? Did having to wait help you to learn patience? Besides helping to learn patience, does having to wait offer any other advantages? Do you appreciate something more if you've had to wait for it? Now try to think of a situation in which you had to wait for something you wanted, but while you waited you decided you really didn't want that something after all. Does waiting help you to re-evaluate what you really want and need? Express your thoughts and ideas on this subject in a composition.

CREATIVE ENCOUNTER #6..........Creative Thinking

NAME ______________________

"I remember hearing Tom Landry, longtime coach of the Dallas Cowboys, speak several years ago after they won their first Super Bowl. He commended the whole team in various ways, but especially one man—Roger Staubach—the successful Cowboy quarterback. 'Roger always puts forth that extra effort,' he said. 'When the men end practice with so many required laps around the field, Roger always makes at least one more than everyone else. He's just that kind of hardworking person,' commented Landry. And, of course, it paid off for Roger Staubach and the whole team."

1. Do you like competition? Why or why not?

2. Describe two experiences in which you won in some type of competition. Describe two experiences in which you lost. How did you feel in each instance?

3. Which is most important to you—winning or just having fun? Why?

4. Pretend you are a coach. Your team has just won the "big game." Write a speech of congratulations to your team.

Creative Encounter #6 continued

5. Now imagine that your team has just lost the "big game." What will you say to console your team members?

____

____

____

____

6. Think of a situation in which someone needs to be consoled or encouraged. Describe the situation, and ask a friend to respond with words of comfort.

Situation:

____

____

____

____

Your friend's response:

____

____

____

____

NAME ____________________

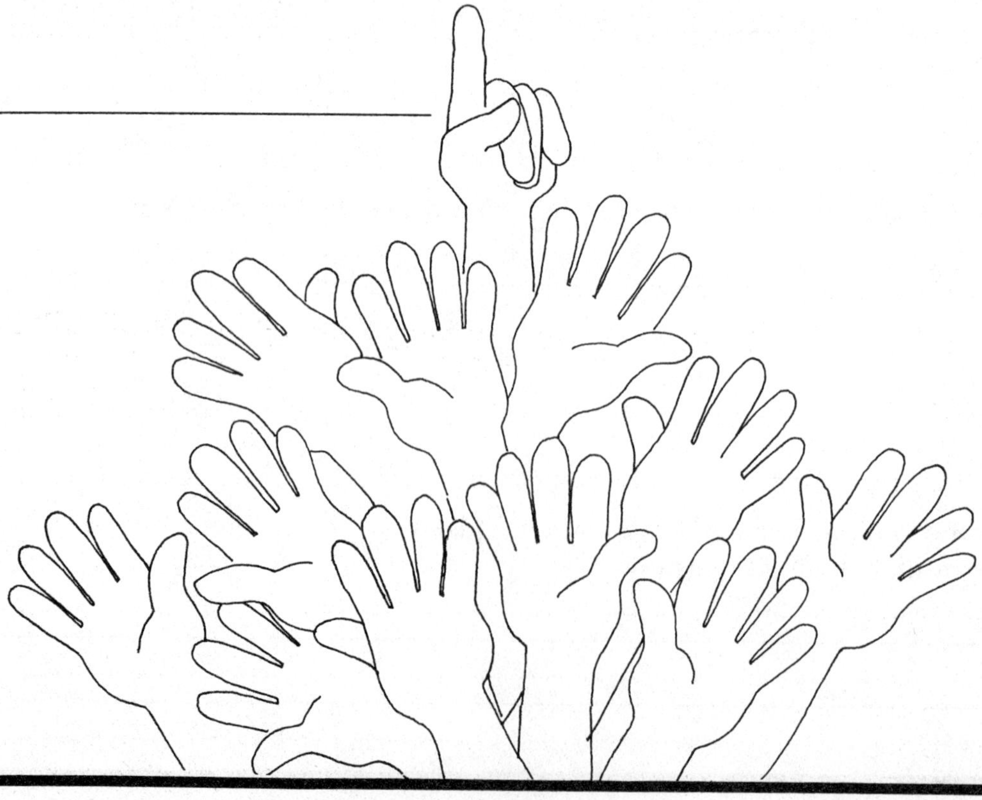

Dr. Getz describes the following words in his books: listening, wisdom, encouragement, perseverance, responsibility, obedience, understanding, joy, self-discipline and patience.

1. List these ten words on a separate sheet of paper. For each word, give a definition (use a dictionary) and write a sentence or phrase telling how each is important in the development of your relationships and in your development as a person. The first word *listening* is done for you as an example.

listening
     definition: the act of making a conscious effort to hear or to attend closely

     role in development:
       of relationships—   Listening carefully to another makes him feel that what he has to say is important to me and that I care about him and value him as a person.

       as a person—   Listening helps me to see that my viewpoint isn't the only one and that there may be other valid ways of looking at things besides my own.

2. If you had to decide which three qualities were most important in the development of your relationships and in your development as a person, which three would you choose? Why? List your choices and reasons for those choices below.

A. _____

_____

_____

_____

B. _____

_____

_____

_____

C. _____

_____

INDEPENDENT PROJECTS—GETZ

1. Dr. Getz has written many books about the family and how to build character and develop friendship. Express your thoughts in creative writing about what constitutes a happy family and how to make friends.

2. *"We are surrounded with opportunities. Even in the midst of our inflationary trends there are still unique opportunities for people from all walks of life and from all kinds of economic backgrounds to better their economic situation. It is possible in America, because it happens,"* states Dr. Getz.

   Think of people who rose from simple backgrounds to extraordinary leadership and prosperity, for example, Colonel Sanders and Michael Faraday. Choose one of these people, prepare a report about him, emphasizing how he achieved success, and present your report to the class.

3. Dr. Getz states, *"One story that has intrigued me is that told by Mary Crowley. Her early years were spent as an orphan. Mary did not have enough money to take care of her own needs. The story that unfolds in her life is incredible. Today Mary Crowley operates a multi-million-dollar enterprise called Home Interiors and Gifts, Inc., located in Dallas, Texas."* Read about the life and philosophy of Mary Crowley.

4. Dr. Getz refers to Eric Liddell's endurance and steadfastness that is illustrated and contrasted in the award-winning film *Chariots of Fire*. Read about the life of Eric Liddell, a runner who set a new Olympic record in the 1924 Olympics. Make a book jacket to illustrate his life.

RESOURCE BOOKS—GETZ

Bjorn, Thyra Ferre. *Dear Papa*. Old Tappan, New Jersey: Fleming H. Revell Co., 1963.

Bjorn, Thyra Ferre. *Papa's Daughter*. New York: Bantam Books, 1958.

Bjorn, Thyra Ferre. *Papa's Wife*. New York: Bantam Books, 1955.

Bjorn, Thyra Ferre. *This Is My Life*. Old Tappan, New Jersey: Fleming H. Revell Co., 1966.

Colson, Charles W. *Life Sentence*. Old Tappan, New Jersey: Fleming H. Revell Co., 1979.

Crowley, Mary C. *You Can Too*. Old Tappan, New Jersey: Fleming H. Revell Co., 1980.

Getz, Gene A. *Building Up One Another*. Wheaton, Illinois: Victor Books, 1976.

Getz, Gene A. *Encouraging One Another*. Wheaton, Illinois: Victor Books, 1976.

Getz, Gene A. *The Measure of a Family*. Glendale, California: Regal Books, 1976.

Magnusson, Sally. *The Flying Scotsman*. New York: Quartet Books, Inc., 1981.

Oke, Janette. *Love Comes Softly*. Minneapolis, Minnesota: Bethany Fellowship, Inc., 1979.

Oke, Janette. *Love's Abiding Joy*. Minneapolis, Minnesota: Bethany House Publishers, 1983.

Oke, Janette. *Love's Enduring Promise*. Minneapolis, Minnesota: Bethany Fellowship, Inc., 1980.

Oke, Janette. *Love's Long Journey*. Minneapolis, Minnesota: Bethany House Publishers, 1982.

Oke, Janette. *When Calls the Heart*. Minneapolis, Minnesota: Bethany House Publishers, 1983.

PETER JENKINS

*"Today the sky was bluer than the ocean just a mile away. The sun was here to congratulate **us** for having made it. All that I'd seen and felt was coming back all at once. What an **incredible** country I'd found . . . . I was glad it was over and I was sad. What this walk meant to me would take a lifetime to understand.*

"We walked thousands of miles and would not have made it without all the people who reached out to us along the way. We would not have been able to experience all that we did without those generous Americans. They gave us food when we needed it and work when we were out of money. There were those who gave us their love, time, support, advice, and their life's story. Some prayed for us.

"I started out searching for myself and my country and found both. Throughout our journey we found an America we loved."

Peter Jenkins

BIOGRAPHICAL SKETCH

As a college student, Peter Jenkins was confused and disillusioned about what he had been hearing about America. Before abandoning his homeland, Peter decided to give the United States one more chance. He decided the way to accomplish that was to walk across America and discover where he and America stood.

On October 15, 1973, he started his walk from Alfred, New York, and arrived at the Oregon coast five and a half years later. Peter and Cooper, his dog, trained for four and a half months, running hundreds of hours uphill and down to prepare for this journey. On that Allegheny autumn morning a crowd of friends walked the first steps of the journey with Peter and Cooper.

Peter Jenkins found it wasn't enough to walk through America, for he wanted to stop, work, and live with the people. He met a mountain man in Virginia, a loving Black family in North Carolina, the governor of Alabama, and many other American heroes. Peter plotted his route by asking directions from farmers, hunters, police, or anyone he met. The death of Cooper beneath a truck left Peter stunned and overwhelmed.

Peter Jenkins decided to write about the first part of his walk at a seminary in New Orleans, where he met Barbara. Later he married this gentle belle, who had never hiked or camped out in her life. With two large golfing umbrellas attached to their backpacks, Peter and Barbara traveled through a land of dust storms, tornadoes, cacti, rattlesnakes, mosquitoes, coyotes, scorpions, and muggers. Across golden prairies and snow-capped mountains, these pioneers faced incredible dangers and adventures.

On January 18, 1979, 150 people, including Barbara's eighty-three-year-old grandmother, walked the final steps with Peter and Barbara. Their last mile felt like all the July Fourths they had ever known.

Experiences during the first part of Peter's journey are recorded in *A Walk Across America*. Barbara joined him for the rest of the journey, and together they wrote *The Walk West*. The two volumes became national best sellers. During his 4,751 mile walk Peter had worn thirty-five pairs of shoes. As a result of this incredible journey, his faith and pride in America were restored.

CREATIVE ENCOUNTER #1.........A Class Discussion

"Before Dad drove away, he pulled me aside and said, 'Son, we are proud of what you are doing. You be sure you treat everyone like you've been treated by these fine people and you will continue to find great Americans everywhere you and Cooper walk.' That bit of wisdom would stay with me forever."

What advice or words of wisdom have you received that have influenced your life?

Describe situations when others have come to you for guidance.

What advice did you give them?

If you could write three sentences of advice that would be published in the newspapers across America, what would you write?

CREATIVE ENCOUNTER #2.........Exploring Your Heritage

Peter and Barbara Jenkins learned from older people, who shared with them their spirit of overcoming, strength, stability, and years of wisdom. Barbara stated, *"They are the kind of people whose voices need to be heard in this country."*

Read the books by Peter Jenkins.

Discuss their experiences with Homer Davenport in Virginia, Oscar and Annie Winkler in North Carolina, and Homer and Ruby Martin in Texas.

Peter and Barbara Jenkins' next book will examine parts of the country they missed. They are asking people to write to them to tell them about their parts of the country and why they enjoy living there.

Write about your part of the country. Interview your grandparents, parents, other relatives, and friends. Include your family background, traditions, photographs, and/or illustrations.

CREATIVE ENCOUNTER #3.........Planning a Trip

"Mileage craziness is a serious condition that exists in many forms. The symptoms may lead to obsessively placing more importance on how many miles are traveled than on the real reason for traveling. On foot, in a van, on a fleet motorcycle or on a bicycle, a person must be very careful not to become overly concerned with arriving.

"My main purpose was to be where I was. Most important, I wanted to find the real people out there, what they were made of, experience who they were, how they lived, and how they worked for a living."

If you could travel anywhere, where would you like to travel?

On a separate sheet of paper, plan a trip.

Decide how much you will spend, where you will stay, and your means of transportation.

What will be the purpose of your trip?

"While we walked so carefree down the lightly traveled country highway, I promised myself we would follow two laws. One is a Sioux law: 'With all beings and all things we shall be as relatives.' My law said, 'Every morning we will leave our campsite as a deer would, with only a few hundred bent blades of grass to show we have been there.' "

Discuss some of the adventures of Cooper, Peter, and Barbara.

What preparation and training is involved for an extensive hike, backpacking, and camping?

Choose a topic to research: clothing, footwear, shelter, safety and first aid, equipment, weather, physical conditioning, building a campfire, outdoor cooking, maps, compasses, survival skills, nature study, fishing, boating, swimming, archery, outdoor activities, parks, or recreation areas. Combine your topic of research with your classmates' topics and make a nature magazine. Include photographs of nature and/or illustrations in your guide to hiking, backpacking, and camping. Use the articles in *National Geographic* as references.

CREATIVE ENCOUNTER #5..........Creative Code

Peter invented a code to record events since living in a tent made it impossible to write detailed journals and notes. The first code that he thought of was KEDD, **K**iller **E**nergy **D**rain **D**ay. This code summarized the second day away from Homer's: 25M, 05-20F, SFW 4-6 in., SN, AL, MCP, FFLH, 3, 3-7.

25M stood for twenty-five miles walked. 05-20F meant the temperature fluctuated between 5 and 20 degrees. SFW meant the snow fell four to six inches and the W stood for a strong blowing wind. SN meant Peter and Cooper slept the night inside. AL and MCP symbolized they both ate little, and he needed maximum clothing protection to stay warm. FFLH represented that his feet felt like hamburger. The last symbols were numbers to grade each day. The physical demands were a little harder than an average 3. The mental stress was easier in the morning so he rated it a 3, but as the snowstorm grew worse, the mental stress increased to a 7.

Research various types of codes and ciphers. Devise your own code and send secret messages.

_____ Your Secret Code _____

_____ Your Secret Message _____

NAME _____

CREATIVE ENCOUNTER #6.........A Creative Recipe

Peter Jenkins talks about his unshakable love for his country. *"Well, sir, for nine months now I've been walking, and I've come to realize what a bad press America's been giving itself. There's a lot of good in it that also needs telling. The land, the geography—they're unbelievable. And the people! I haven't gone a day that someone I met hasn't been kind, or thoughtful, or helpful. Plain, simple, ordinary folks they may be, but they're heroes to me.*

"The people who mingled their lives with ours were just ordinary Americans—the ones whose working hands and loving hearts make this country—literally."

Create a recipe of characteristics that make America. For example, 7 cups of patriotism, 3 pints of freedom, and 6 tablespoons of generosity. Write your recipe in calligraphy below. Extend this activity by creating your recipes about family, home, and friends.

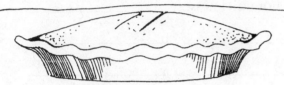

Recipe: Parents' Pie
From the kitchen of children who love their parents

10 lbs. of We Love You
10 gal. of Obedience
5 cups of Hugs and Kisses
6 tsp. of Laughter
7 cups of Understanding
8 1/2 cups of Respect
5 scoops of Generosity
3 1/2 tsp. of Joy
5 cups of Truth
3 dashes of Trouble
2 tsp. of Sorrow (optional)
So quickly stir in 5 cups of Forgiveness
1 tsp. of Behavior
8 cups of Together Time
6 cups of Helping
5 pinches of Smiles
6 oz. of Fun

Mix it together and you'll discover our gift from the children who love their parents!!

CREATIVE ENCOUNTER #7..........Appreciating America

The roughest part of walking across America was the difficult good-byes. Peter felt that Cooper's tremendous love, energy, and unchained freedom had captured life itself. When Peter buried his companion, he grieved deeply and walked alone. On their walk, Peter and Barbara Jenkins experienced the adjustments of loss of loved ones, moving, homesickness, good-byes, exhaustion, physical pain, and many emotions. However, after they said their good-byes to close friends, they soon discovered new opportunities and people, which added enlightening dimensions to their lives.

1. Describe an experience in your own life when you had to say good-bye. _____

   _____

   _____

2. Describe a situation in which you experienced homesickness. _____

   _____

   _____

3. What did you do to overcome these feelings of loneliness? (meet new friends, participate in activities) _____

   _____

   _____

4. After you said good-bye, what new opportunities did you encounter? (new school, new skills) _____

   _____

   _____

5. How have the experiences and lives of Peter and Barbara Jenkins influenced your life? _____

   _____

   _____

6. How have they helped you gain a new appreciation for America? _____

   _____

   _____

7. Express your thoughts about America in creative writing.

   _____

   _____

8. Give a speech entitled "What I Can Do for My Country."

CREATIVE ENCOUNTER #8..........Your Walk Across America

Imagine that you're planning to walk across America. On the map below, fill in the name of each state. Mark your starting point and show the route you will take. Also, indicate places along the way where you'd like to stop and spend some time. Include any special illustrations you desire, such as animals, scenery, landmarks, interesting people, etc.

Why did you choose this particular route?

How long do you expect your walk to take?

What special problems might you encounter along the way? When your map is completed, compare it with the maps of your classmates.

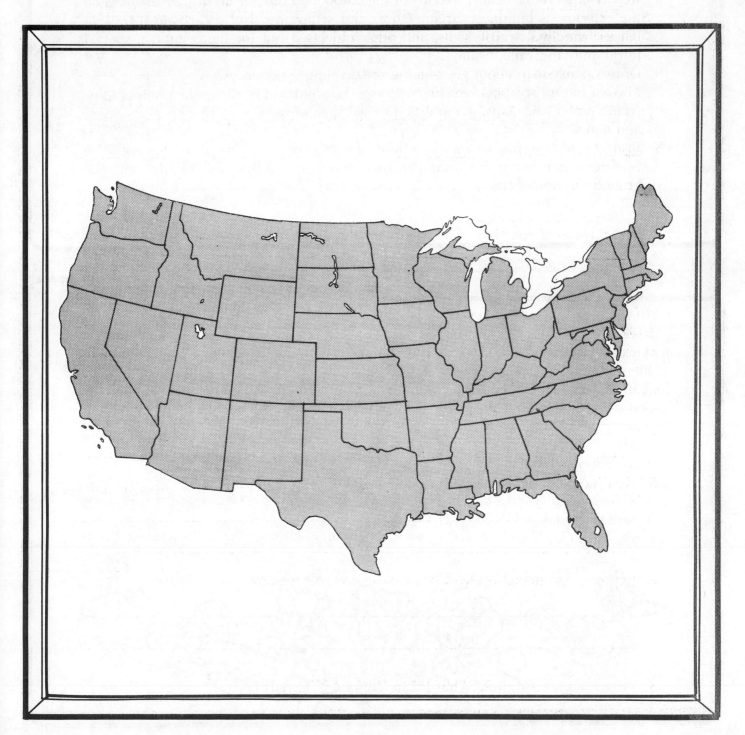

INDEPENDENT PROJECTS—JENKINS

1. Discuss the opinions of Peter Jenkins about the news media in America and his transition from a lack of hope to a dedicated love for America. Conduct a debate about the power and control of the news media.
2. Create a diorama of scenery in America.
3. Cooper Half Malamute, a loyal companion, helped to defend and save Peter's life in times of danger. Research the training and care of pets. Share experiences about your own pets.
4. Find poetry that uses nature imagery. Give an oral interpretation in an outdoor drama.
5. Keenly observe the beauty and art of the outdoors. Look for decorative art used on the exterior of buildings, architecture, and sculptures. Notice artistic details in fences, windows, traffic signs, and other objects. Hunt for the beauty in special floral and landscape displays.
6. Draw a story map about your hiking or traveling experiences.
7. Make a nature scrapbook or diary of your family trips. Arrange the photographs, scenic postcards, maps, pamphlets, pressed specimens of wild flowers and leaves, and notes.
8. Brainstorm: Use your ingenuity to think of materials found in nature that could be used for camp living. For example, find sturdy forked branches to stick into the ground for clothes trees.

RESOURCE BOOKS—JENKINS

Gardner, Martin. *Codes, Ciphers and Secret Writing.* New York: Simon and Schuster, 1972.

Jenkins, Peter. "A Walk Across America." *National Geographic*, April 1977, pp. 466-499.

Jenkins, Peter. "The Walk West." *National Geographic*, August 1979, pp. 194-229.

Jenkins, Peter. *A Walk Across America.* New York: Fawcett Crest Books, 1979.

Jenkins, Peter, and Barbara Jenkins.. *The Walk West.* New York: Fawcett Crest Books, 1981.

Larson, Randy. *Backpacking.* New York: Harvey House, Publishers, 1979.

Ledlie, John A., ed. *Camping Skills for Trail Living.* New York: Association Press, 1962.

Lyttle, Richard B. *The Complete Beginner's Guide to Backpacking.* Garden City, New York: Doubleday & Co., Inc., 1975.

Merrill, Bill. *The Hiker's and Backpacker's Handbook.* New York: Winchester Press, 1971.

HELEN KELLER

"Thus I learned from life itself. At the beginning I was only a little mass of possibilities. It was my teacher who unfolded and developed them. When she came, everything about me breathed of love and joy and was full of meaning. She has never since let pass an opportunity to point out the beauty that is in everything, nor has she ceased trying in thought and action and example to make my life sweet and useful.

"Out of the orb of darkness she led me into golden hours and regions of beauteous thought, bright-spun of love and dreams. Thought-buds opened softly in the walled garden of my mind. Love flowered sweetly in my heart. Spring sang joyously in all the silent, hidden nooks of childhood, and the dark night of blindness shone with the glory of stars unseen. As she opened the locked gates of my being my heart leapt with gladness and my feet felt the thrill of the chanting sea. Happiness flooded my being as the sun overflows the earth, and I stretched out my hands in quest of life."

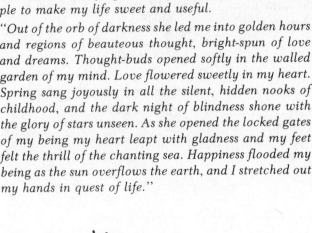

BIOGRAPHICAL SKETCH

Helen was a vivacious child who at the age of nineteen months was stricken by a severe illness that left her blind, deaf, and mute. Endowed with an alert and active mind, Helen fought furiously to free herself from a world of silence and darkness.

Helen's mother read about the education of Laura Bridgman, a deaf and blind child. This gave the Keller family new hope. Helen's father took her to Dr. Alexander Graham Bell. He advised Mr. Keller to write to the Perkins Institution for the Blind in Boston to find a teacher for Helen.

Shortly before Helen was seven, Anne Sullivan arrived from Boston. Laura Bridgman warned Anne not to spoil Helen by letting her become disobedient. Later Anne wrote, *"I suppose I shall have many such battles with the little woman before she learns the only two essential things I can teach her, obedience and love."*

Anne was able to communicate with Helen through touch. She spelled words into Helen's hand. Gradually, Helen was able to connect words with objects. The day she spelled and understood the word *water* Helen describes as her mental awakening and when her endless quest for knowledge began.

Helen seemed to sense the state of mind of those around her. When she entered a greenhouse, her face would light up as she recognized each flower by its fragrance and touch. Since she could feel sounds through her hands and feet, she could understand music through the vibrations made by various instruments.

In 1904 Helen graduated from Radcliffe College cum laude; after graduating she wrote, lectured, and traveled to help meet the needs of the deaf, blind, and other handicapped people.

Helen told Anne, *"I must teach people what you taught me—that children must not be different because they are blind and deaf. They can learn to work and be happy."*

CREATIVE ENCOUNTER #1..........Showing Appreciation

"It was my teacher's genius, her quick sympathy, her loving tact which made the first years of my education so beautiful. It was because she seized the right moment to impart knowledge that made it so pleasant and acceptable to me. She realized that a child's mind is like a shallow brook which ripples and dances merrily over the stony course of its education and reflects here a flower, there a bush, yonder a fleecy cloud; and she attempted to guide my mind on its way, knowing that like a brook it should be fed by mountain streams and hidden springs, until it broadened out into a deep river, capable of reflecting in its placid surface billowy hills, the luminous shadows of trees and the blue heavens, as well as the sweet face of a little flower."

1. Share some things for which you are thankful. _____

    _____

    _____

    _____

    _____

    _____

    _____

2. How have special people influenced your life? _____

    _____

    _____

    _____

    _____

    _____

3. Show your appreciation to these people by writing a note of thanks or performing other deeds of thanksgiving. In the space provided, describe what you plan to do.

    _____

    _____

    _____

    _____

4. On the back design a certificate of appreciation for a special person in your life.

CREATIVE ENCOUNTER #2..........Smiles, Sunshine, and Love

Anne Sullivan spelled into Helen's hand: *"I love you."* Helen quickly inquired, *"What is love?"*

Later in her life Helen talked about love. *"Silence sits immense upon my soul. Then comes hope with a smile and whispers, 'There is joy in self-forgetfulness.' So I try to make the light in others' eyes my sun, the music in others' ears my symphony, the smile on others' lips my happiness.*

"Life is an exciting business and most exciting when lived for others. I thank God for my handicaps for through them I have found myself, my work, and my God. When one door of happiness closes, another opens; but often we look so long at the closed door that we do not see the one which has been opened for us."

Tell what you think Helen meant by *"There is joy in self-forgetfulness."*

Express your thoughts about love, joy and hope in a creative composition.

CREATIVE ENCOUNTER #3..........A Class Discussion

Helen Keller's friend Mark Twain said, *"Helen, the world is full of unseeing eyes, vacant, staring, soulless eyes."*

When Helen was twelve years old, she was falsely accused of plagiarism. Later Helen said, *"I think if this sorrow had come to me when I was older, it would have broken my spirit beyond repairing."*

Mr. Gilman, the principal, believed that Helen should lengthen her stay at Cambridge School, because her presence gave his school wide publicity. From the evidence, it seemed Mr. Gilman wanted to separate Anne from Helen and take charge of Helen's education for his own fame. He wrote letters to Helen's benefactors that accused Anne of mistreating and cruelly overworking Helen. Mr. Gilman had deviously convinced Mrs. Keller to authorize him to act as Helen's guardian. Helen, who was seventeen years old, wrestled with agony, fear, and despair because her beloved teacher was falsely insulted, betrayed, and driven from her.

Helen stated, *"Now our worst worry is over, and nothing could have induced me to put it down in written words if I had been the only person to suffer. I should have buried it in the depths of silence. But my teacher and I have been plunged into this misery; we have struggled together through a maze of falsehood and injustice, and we have landed on the firm, safe stand of Right and Justice. Nevertheless, I feel that I ought to make a statement of our sorrow; so that all my friends may know the real truth, and understand that my dear, faithful teacher has never, never deserved the cruel things that Mr. Gilman has said about her. I know now that men can be false and wicked, even while they seem kind and true. I have found that I cannot always put my hand in another's with a trustful spirit. Yet I know that goodness is mightier than evil, and my heart still tells me that love is the most beautiful thing in the whole world and must triumph in the end."*

What valuable lessons have you learned from Helen's experience?

Describe an experience when you were falsely accused.

What advice would you give to the one who is falsely accused?

Discuss deceiving situations in life similar to Helen's experiences.

How did Helen overcome her painful experiences?

How do you believe one can successfully cope with these situations?

CREATIVE ENCOUNTER #4.........Enjoying Nature

Helen loved nature and animals. Anne introduced her at an early age to the zoo. Helen climbed on an elephant, played with a monkey, patted a lion, and felt the ears of a giraffe. She enjoyed the country, horseback riding, winter sleigh rides, and sitting in their tree house. Dogs were her friends.

1. Describe the touch of a puppy to someone who is paralyzed, who cannot feel.

   _____

   _____

   _____

2. Wear a blindfold and jog in place. Describe the feeling after jogging. _____

   _____

   _____

3. Close your eyes. Let your imagination go. Imagine yourself exploring and climbing in the mountains. Describe the scenery of snow-covered mountains to someone who cannot. Use adjectives and two or three-word phrases. _____

   _____

   _____

   _____

4. Draw the sound of a waterfall to someone who cannot hear.

5. Describe the sound of a bird singing.

   _____

   _____

   _____

6. Describe the taste of an orange.

   _____

   _____

7. Describe the smell of a rose.

   _____

   _____

CREATIVE ENCOUNTER #5.........Group Discussion

"I feel the delicate symmetry of a leaf. I pass my hands lovingly about the smooth skin of a silver birch, or the rough shaggy bark of a pine. In spring I touch the branches of trees hopefully in search of a bud, the first sign of awakening nature after her winter's sleep. Occasionally, if I am fortunate, I place my hand gently on a small tree and feel the happy quiver of a bird in full song."

"Listen" to the sounds of springtime. Use your hands to help you describe these sounds to someone who cannot hear.

"Listen" to a sunset. Describe the sun setting in the majestic mountains, fertile plains, lush forest, awe-inspiring desert, or near a magnificent ocean. Describe this scene to someone who cannot see. Be creative. You are helping someone to "see" with his/her ears.

Discuss the five senses with new appreciation.

Close your eyes. Imagine the world of a blind person. Hand an object to a friend whose eyes are closed and ask him to guess what it is. Describe this experience.

How is a blind person dependent on his other senses?

Close your eyes and plug your ears. Imagine the world of Helen Keller. Describe this experience. Now observe and listen carefully to your surrounding sights and sounds. How has Helen Keller's life made you appreciate the little things in life?

Hands
by
Anne Sullivan
Hands, understanding hands,
Hands that caress like delicate green leaves,
Hands, eager hands,
Hands that gather knowledge from great books-
Braille Books-
Hands that fill empty space with livable things,
Hands so quiet, folded on a book-
Hands forgetful of words they have read all night,
Hands asleep on the open page,
Strong hands that sew and reap thought,
Hands tremulous and ecstatic listening to music
Hands keeping the rhythm of song and dance.

CREATIVE ENCOUNTER #6.........A Creative Composition

"I who am blind can give one hint to those who see: use your eyes as if tomorrow you would be stricken blind. And the same method can be applied to the other senses."

"Hear the music of voices, the song of a bird, the mighty strains of an orchestra as if you would be stricken deaf tomorrow. Touch each object as if tomorrow your tactile sense would fail. Smell the perfume of flowers, taste with relish each morsel as if tomorrow you could never smell and taste again. Make the most of every sense, glory in all the facets of pleasure and beauty which the world reveals to you through the several means of contact which nature provides. But of all the senses, I am sure that sight must be far and away the most delightful."

Helen wrote an article entitled "Three Days to See."

How would you use your eyes if you had just three more days to see?

Express your thoughts about this in a creative composition.

INDEPENDENT PROJECTS—KELLER

1. Research the following topic: How can we meet the needs of the handicapped? Describe your experiences with handicapped people. Make a poster of guidelines on how one should relate to the deaf, blind, and other handicapped people.
2. Give an oral presentation about the training of seeing-eye dogs.
3. Investigate career opportunities in working with the handicapped. Make a chart about your research.
4. Learn the manual alphabet and sign language.
5. Invite a person who knows sign language to your class. Sing songs in sign language.
6. Dramatize with majestic actions to express the sound and message of "America, the Beautiful." Describe the music with sign language to someone who cannot hear.
7. Read about the difficult childhood of Anne Sullivan. Write about her training and the teaching techniques she used with Helen Keller.

RESOURCE BOOKS—KELLER

Bigland, Eileen. *Helen Keller.* New York: S.G. Phillips, Inc., 1967.

Gadling, Donna C., Daniel H. Pokorny, and Lottie L. Riekehof. *Lift Up Your Hands: Inspirational and Patriotic Songs in the Language of Signs.* Washington, D.C.: The National Grange, 1976.

Harrity, Richard, and Ralph G. Martin. *The Three Lives of Helen Keller.* Garden City, New York: Doubleday & Co., Inc., 1962.

Hickok, Lorena A. *The Story of Helen Keller.* New York: Grosset & Dunlap, 1958.

Hickok, Lorena A. *The Touch of Magic: The Story of Helen Keller's Great Teacher Anne Sullivan Macy.* New York: Dodd, Mead & Co., 1961.

Keller, Helen. *Midstream: My Later Life.* Garden City, New York: Doubleday, Doran & Co., Inc., 1929.

Keller, Helen. *The Story of My Life.* Garden City, New York: Doubleday & Co., Inc., 1902.

Keller, Helen. *Teacher Anne Sullivan Macy.* Garden City, New York: Doubleday & Co., Inc., 1955.

Peare, Catherine Owens. *The Helen Keller Story.* New York: Thomas Y. Crowell Co., 1959.

Richards, Norman. *People of Destiny: Helen Keller.* Chicago: Children's Press, 1968.

Riekehof, Lottie L. *The Joy of Signing: The New Illustrated Guide for Mastering Sign Language and the Manual Alphabet.* Springfield, Missouri: Gospel Publishing House, 1978.

DAVID LIVINGSTONE

"If roads were laid down and communication made easy their mutual fears might end. And if a route could be mapped across the continent, then the people of Africa and people of other lands could meet, trade goods and ideas, and everyone would be richer and wiser.

"I have laboured in bricks and mortar, at the forge and carpenter's bench, as well as in preaching and medical practice. I like this traveling very much indeed. There is so much freedom in our African manners. We pitch our tent, make our fire, wherever we choose; walk, ride, or shoot at game, as our inclination leads us; but there is a great drawback—we can't study or read as we please.

"Nature is full of enjoyment. I can be rich without money. Let us appear just what we are. Choose a path by which you will be able by your exertions to benefit the world, and bend your energies to that."

David Livingstone

BIOGRAPHICAL SKETCH

Born in a small village in Scotland, David grew up in a poor, hardworking family whose members had a zeal for education and a sense of mission. As one of seven children, David was reared in a single room at the top of a tenement building for the workers of a cotton factory. At the age of ten he worked from six in the morning until eight at night at a local cotton factory to help support his family. With part of his first week's wages he bought a Latin grammar, which he propped up on his machine so that he could memorize the Latin words and phrases. In the following years, he learned to shut out the noise of the machinery while he studied Greek, medicine, and theology. He went to evening school and then studied at home by candlelight.

"Looking back on that life of toil," he wrote years later, *"I cannot but feel thankful that it formed such a material part of my education; and were it possible I should like to begin life over again in the same lowly style, and pass through the same training."*

David was fascinated by nature and the subject of geography. Roaming the countryside, he studied wildflowers and nature and came home with his pockets full of plants and rocks. The foundations for much of his later work as an explorer were laid in his home country.

David Livingstone was twenty-eight years old when he arrived at Cape Town on March 14, 1841. Among the hardships of mapping an unknown land were hostile natives, slave traders, poor health, flooded rivers, barren deserts, and forest fires. During a journey to establish a mission station, he was attacked by a lion. Two natives rushed to the rescue and killed the lion, but he never again had full, free use of his left arm.

In 1853 Dr. Livingstone made his purpose clear: *"I shall open up a path into the interior, or perish."* In his thirty years of heroic work in Africa, he traveled thousands of miles and charted routes into the interior, which opened the continent to the world.

The African natives were devoted to Dr. Livingstone and called him "father," "the great master," and "the good one." He was a missionary, physician, explorer, geographer, zoologist, botanist, scientist, linguist, astronomer, chemist, and mercantile director. In the face of danger and trials, Dr. David Livingstone portrayed enduring faith, courage, long-suffering, and service.

CREATIVE ENCOUNTER #1..........An Adventurous Journey

"The prospect of a highway, capable of being traversed by boats to an entirely unexplored and very populous region, grew from that time forward stronger and stronger in my mind; so much so, that when we actually came to the lake, this idea occupied such a large portion of my mental vision that the actual discovery seemed of but little importance."

Let your imagination go. Imagine yourself floating on water. There are no flowers, no trees, no land in sight. A family of dolphins looks at you curiously. Fish are surrounding you. The sun is glaring. The waves are tossing you up and down, back and forth. Then suddenly, there's hope! An island is in sight! What did you say or think when you arrived on shore?

Examine the map of the island below. This island is about 20 miles wide and 30 miles long. Where is this island? Using longitude and latitude, locate this area on a globe. What kind of climate does this island have? What other places have similar climates?

On the map, mark the site where you landed and the area in which you settled.

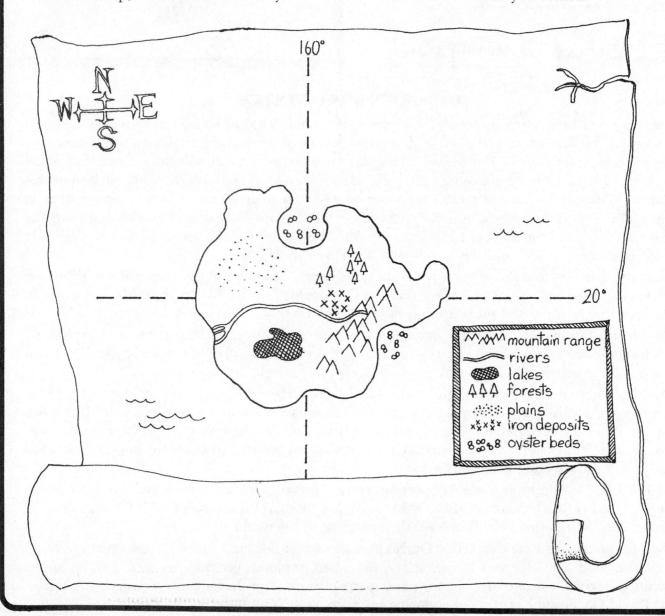

CREATIVE ENCOUNTER #2..........Exploring an Island

Explore the features of the island. Using research and map skills, plan your survival. You have only a knife as a tool. The questions are a guide for you. First complete these questions individually. Then share your adventures and ideas with your group.

1. How did you get to this island? What happened to you before you arrived on this island?

2. Where did you land?

3. Where will you settle? Why?

4. Where will you find food? List what you will eat.

5. What will the weather be like?

6. What natural resources does this island have?

7. How will you use the natural resources? How will they help you survive?

8. How will you build shelter? How will you cut down trees?

9. Write a diary of how you survived for the first two weeks.

10. What animals do you encounter?

11. What will you name this island?

12. Where will farms be established? Why?

13. Where will you build your first community? Why?

14. How will you establish a government?

15. Where will you build roads? Do you plan to attract tourists? If so, design your tourist attractions.

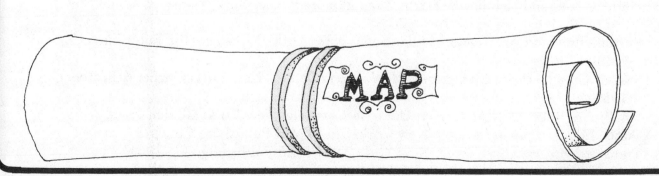

INDEPENDENT PROJECTS— LIVINGSTONE

1. Design your own map of an island.
2. If you could be an explorer, where would you like to explore? Keep a diary of your adventures and explorations.
3. Outline specific directions for a treasure hunt.
4. Make a poster and display of camping equipment and survival skills.
5. Produce a news broadcast about the discovery and early settlement of the land near your home.
6. Design a post card and a brochure about the history, natural resources, industry, prominent people, landmarks, parks, and recreation of your state that would attract visitors.
7. Research the life and exploration of Daniel Boone and other American explorers. Sketch the routes of their expeditions.
8. Read about the lives of explorers and/or pioneers. Write a journal from the viewpoint of an explorer or pioneer.
9. Plan an archaeological dig and expedition.
10. Make a puppet of a well-known explorer or other person. Glue your drawing on cardboard and attach the figure to a stick. Dramatically present your puppet with a speaking part that portrays your character. Introduce your puppet to those made by other students and then discuss life experiences, talents, and interests of each.
11. Make a documentary filmstrip about your research of life in Africa.

RESOURCE BOOKS—LIVINGSTONE

Arnold, Richard. *The True Story of David Livingstone, Explorer.* Chicago: Children's Press, 1964.

Coffman, Ramon Peyton, and Nathan G. Goodman. *Famous Explorers for Young People.* New York: Dodd, Mead, & Co., 1945.

Cottler, Joseph, and Haym Jaffe. *Heroes of Civilization.* Boston: Little, Brown and Co., 1969.

Eaton, Jeanette. *David Livingstone: Foe of Darkness.* New York: William Morrow & Co., 1947.

Gilbert, Miriam. *This Is My Country: A Child's Pictorial Guide to the United States.* New York: The Lion Press, Inc., 1968.

Grosseck, Joyce, and Elizabeth Attwood. *Great Explorers.* Grand Rapids, Michigan: The Fideler Co., 1981.

Hillcourt, William. *The New Field Book of Nature Activities and Hobbies.* New York: G.P. Putnam's Sons, 1970.

Hoff, Rhoda, and Helmut de Terra. *They Explored!* New York: Henry Z. Walck, Inc., 1959.

Purton, Rowland W. *Doctor Livingstone.* New York: McGraw-Hill Publishing Co., Limited, 1968.

Seaver, George. *David Livingstone: His Life and Letters.* New York: Harper & Brothers, 1957.

Smallman, Robert E. *The Golden Guide to Camping.* New York: Golden Press, 1965.

Tunis, Edwin. *Colonial Living.* New York: The World Publishing Co., 1957.

Tunis, Edwin. *Frontier Living.* New York: The World Publishing Co., 1961.

WOLFGANG AMADEUS MOZART

"Parents take pains to put their children in a position to earn their own bread, and the children are under an obligation to themselves. The greater the talents they have received from God, the greater obligation to make use of them for the improvement of their own and their parents' circumstances, to assist their parents, and to provide for their own advancement and for the future. The gospel teaches us this usury of talents. I am, therefore, bound before God in my conscience, with all my power to be grateful to my father, who has unweariedly devoted all his time to my education."

BIOGRAPHICAL SKETCH

Johannes Chrysostomus Wolfgangus Theophilus Sigismundus Mozart was known as the "Wonder Child." Seven children were born to Leopold and Anna Maria Mozart, but only two of them lived, Nannerl and Wolfgang. When Nannerl was seven, her father began to cultivate her musical tendency by instructing her on the harpsichord. During his sister's lesson time, three-year-old Wolfgang listened attentively, and then he amused himself by picking out chords on the harpsichord.

Leopold Mozart, an accomplished musician, recognized his son's natural talent and dedicated himself to training his children when they were very young. Wolfgang was four when his father found him composing a concerto. Shortly before Wolfgang's sixth birthday, he, his father and sister made their first music tour.

Wolfgang composed his first minuet at the age of five, his first symphony at eight, and his first opera at twelve. When Wolfgang was thirteen, his first violin sonatas were published in Paris and his first symphonies were performed in London. While touring Italy at age fourteen, he wrote and directed the performance of his opera.

This child prodigy manifested a gentle, sensitive, deeply affectionate nature; he was a serious, thoughtful, and earnest child. Fighting against illness, pain, poverty, debts, jealous rivals, and other trying circumstances, he continued his musical efforts. Even while he was very sick in bed, his active mind could not rest, and he composed. During his lifetime of thirty-five years, he wrote over 600 musical works. Joseph Haydn told Leopold Mozart that he regarded his friend Wolfgang Amadeus Mozart to be *"the greatest composer I know either personally or by name."*

CREATIVE ENCOUNTER #1.........A Class Discussion

"You know that I am, so to speak, soaked in music, that I am immersed in it all day long, and that I love to plan works, study, and meditate. I have an inexpressible desire to write an opera again—composition is my one and only passion and joy. I only have to hear an opera or go into a theater and hear them tuning up to be almost beside myself."

Listen to a few of Wolfgang Amadeus Mozart's compositions.

If you could compose at the age of five, how would you feel about your talent? Would you want to share your talent? Why or why not? The Mozart family toured Europe and performed for royalty, musicians, and scientists, who gave them gifts and honors. Would you want to travel and perform for hundreds of people? Would you like the fame? Why or why not?

When have others watched you perform? For example, you might have had an audience while you were playing basketball, giving a speech, or playing a musical instrument. What are techniques that help you perform in front of other people? How do you deal with stage fright? Practice helps to build self-confidence and develops dexterity and control.

CREATIVE ENCOUNTER #2.........Accepting Yourself

"It is important that there should be a home-life for me specially devoted to my children. God has given them such talent as, setting aside my obligations as a father, would incite me to sacrifice everything to their good education. Every moment that I lose is lost forever; and if I ever knew how valuable time is in youth I know it now. You know that my children are used to work. If they were to get into idle habits on the pretext that one thing or another hindered them my whole structure would fall to the ground. Habit is an iron path, and you know yourself how much my Wolfgang has still to learn."

This was part of a letter written by Leopold Mozart, Wolfgang's father.

Do you have realistic or unrealistic expectations of yourself? Do you feel you need to live up to other people's expectations? Do you feel other people have higher expectations for you than you do for yourself? Do you have a tendency to be a perfectionist? If you strive to achieve an A but only make a B, do you have trouble accepting yourself? How do you react when you make a mistake? Tell if you agree or disagree with the following statement: "If I cannot do something really well, there is little point in trying it." Tell what you think of the following statements: "You will be loved if . . . ." "You will be accepted and approved of when . . . ."

Accept yourself for who you are, not only for the things you do. Do not dwell on your mistakes. Learn from your mistakes and go forward. Don't give up. Balance is a key word. Try to keep your expectations balanced with your strengths and limitations to develop into a well-rounded individual. Believe in yourself. You are a valuable person with special gifts and talents.

CREATIVE ENCOUNTER #3.........A Musical Story

"Ah, if we only had some clarinets, too! You cannot imagine the glorious effect of a symphony with flutes, oboes, and clarinets!" Wolfgang Amadeus Mozart wrote this in a letter to his father, December 3, 1778.

If you could compose a song, what would it be about and what would you entitle it?

Write a story using instruments for a musical background. For example, use a tambourine for the sound effects of a thundering waterfall or a drum for the sound effects of mysterious footsteps.

While the introduction is being read, close your eyes and think about being a musical instrument. Become an instrument in your imagination. Respond to the questions as though you are a musical instrument.

Imagine musical instruments as the artist's palette. A melody is like a pencil drawing with a shape, pattern and design. The instruments give the composition color. You can color a song light with flutes, dark with violins, or bright with trumpets. You can mix instruments together, like a piano and a harp, to create paintings of a gentle, serene rainbow of colors, or you can mix guitars and an organ to create a sparkling, luminous rainbow of colors. The colors and combinations of colors are fascinating.

1. What musical instrument are you?
2. What instruments are you using to paint your picture of music? What kind of music are you playing?
3. Observe and listen to the other instruments. What do you think are the most interesting features about the other instruments?
4. Practice. Practice. Practice. Your performer has not practiced today. How do you feel?
5. What is your advice to someone who is a beginner in music and chooses you as a musical instrument?
6. You have rehearsed for many hours on your compositions. You and the other instruments are ready to perform. The curtain is up. The spotlight is on you for your solo. How do you feel in the spotlight?
7. You have a very important role in the band or orchestra. Your personality blends harmoniously with the personalities of the other instruments. How do you feel about blending together with the other instruments?
8. Who would you like to have in your audience?
9. The audience is giving you a standing ovation. What do you consider the most outstanding feature about yourself?
10. You have magnificently contributed to the world of sound and color. How could you help others with your songs and music?

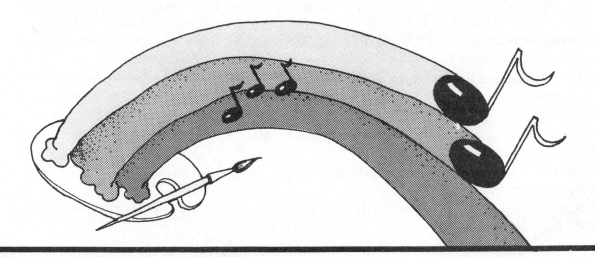

INDEPENDENT PROJECTS—MOZART

1. Practice your musical instrument. Share your talent with senior citizens or younger children.
2. Investigate the roles and characteristics of musical instruments. Make a poster with descriptions and illustrations of musical instruments.
3. Make your own musical instruments.
4. Learn the techniques and motions used to direct a band or chorus.
5. Study music throughout history. Choose a certain period of history, and write about the various styles of music during that time.
6. Research the lives of Handel, Bach, Haydn, and other musicians. Search for the stories behind their compositions.
7. Organize a Music Appreciation Day. Plan a musical presentation about your research and listen to the compositions of the musicians.
8. Plan a recital. Practice your musical instrument. Perform your masterpiece for the recital. If you do not play a musical instrument, sing, be the master of ceremonies, organize the recital, or give an oral interpretation.

RESOURCE BOOKS—MOZART

Bishop, Claire Huchet. *Mozart: Music Magician.* Champaign, Illinois: Garrard Publishing Co., 1968.

Cunningham, Dale. *Picture Book of Music and Its Makers.* New York: Sterling Publishing Co., Inc., 1963.

Kupferberg, Herbert. *A Rainbow of Sound: The Instruments of the Orchestra and Their Music.* New York: Charles Scribner's Sons, 1973.

Mandell, Muriel, and Robert E. Wood. *Make Your Own Musical Instruments.* New York: Sterling Publishing Co., Inc., 1957.

Mirsky, Reba Paeff. *Mozart.* Chicago: Follett Publishing Co., 1960.

Monjo, F. N. *Letters to Horseface, being the story of Wolfgang Amadeus Mozart's journey to Italy 1769-1770, when he was a boy of fourteen.* New York: The Viking Press, 1975.

Shippen, Katherine B., and Anca Seidlova. *The Heritage of Music.* New York: The Viking Press, 1963.

Siegmeister, Elie. *Invitation to Music.* New York: Harvey House, Inc., 1961.

Stearns, Monroe. *Wolfgang Amadeus Mozart: Master of Pure Music.* New York: Franklin Watts, Inc., 1968.

Wechsberg, Joseph. *The Pantheon Story of Music for Young People.* New York: Pantheon Books, 1968.

Wheeler, Opal, and Sybil Deucher: *Mozart: The Wonder Boy.* New York: E. P. Dutton & Co., Inc., 1934.

ISAAC NEWTON

"If I have seen farther it is by standing on the shoulders of giants. I do not know what I may appear to the world; but to myself I seem to have been only like a boy playing on the seashore and diverting myself in now and then finding a smoother pebble or a prettier shell than ordinary, whilst the great ocean of Truth lay all undiscovered before me."

BIOGRAPHICAL SKETCH

Born in a village in England, Isaac was underweight and physically weak, and there were doubts that he would live. His father died before Isaac was born, and at the age of two Isaac was sent to live with his grandmother. He was a quiet, serious, thoughtful child with an unusual ability to concentrate.

According to a statement made late in his life, he was very inattentive in school. His preoccupation with building his intricate mechanical toys caused him to be the lowest in his class. A bully who was ahead of Isaac in the class started a fight with him. Isaac was determined to beat him in his studies and soon rose to be first in his school. Isaac set aside his mechanical toys only when his top-ranking status in school was threatened. This casual attitude about school irritated his teachers.

When Isaac's stepfather died, his mother wanted Isaac, who was sixteen years old, to leave school in order to assume management of the farm. However, he neglected the duties on the farm because he became very absorbed in reading, daydreaming, and designing mechanical models. His teacher, who had recognized Isaac's intellectual gifts, persuaded his mother to send him back to school.

Isaac Newton entered Trinity College at Cambridge University. In 1665, the university closed due to an outbreak of the bubonic plague. During these two years at home on the farm, Isaac made spectacular discoveries in three distinct subjects: calculus, light, and gravitation. He recorded his first thought on gravitation by observing the fall of an apple in the orchard.

Isaac Newton was so absorbed in his work that he often skipped his meals and sleep. His persistence and attention to minute details were remarkable, and he attributed much of his success to staying with a problem until it was solved. He was sensitive to criticism and the scientific arguments that arose from his discoveries. Because he was often unwilling to publish his findings, his friends had to plead with him to publish his most valuable discoveries.

After his graduation, Isaac Newton became a professor of mathematics at Cambridge. He was appointed Master of the British Mint, became a member of Parliament, president of the Royal Society, and was knighted by Queen Anne. His *Principia* established the fundamental laws of modern physics. He published *Opticks*, the result of his experiments and studies in color and light. Sir Isaac Newton was a mathematician, scientist, physicist, astronomer, and natural philosopher, who taught mankind how to discover new truths.

CREATIVE ENCOUNTER #1.........A Class Discussion

As a boy, Isaac's inventions included a sundial, water clock, and a windmill. When he flew a kite with a lantern tied to its tail, the frightened neighbors thought it was a comet.

Isaac's early inventiveness and expertise in mechanics, designing, and manual dexterity assisted his later discoveries. He enjoyed reading, experimenting, devising games, and making models and gadgets.

What are your hobbies?

What are your homemade inventions?

If you had one hour of free time, what would you enjoy doing?

What interests do you and Isaac Newton have in common?

CREATIVE ENCOUNTER #2.........Math and Nature

Albert Einstein wrote this statement about Newton: *"Nature to him was an open book, whose letters he could read without effort."*

Brainstorm: What are all the mathematical relationships and geometric shapes that you can think of that are found in nature?

Here are examples: There is always an even number of rows of seeds running lengthwise on an ear of corn. A honeycomb cross section consists of a series of hexagons.

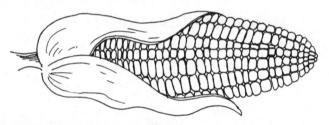

CREATIVE ENCOUNTER #3.........Creative Thinking

In 1926, Wallas, a researcher, proposed the following four main stages in the creative process:

a. Preparation is the stage of investigation, identification of the problem, and a gathering of the facts.

b. Incubation is the stage of reorganization, associating new information with past information. This mental process seems to happen without the individual being directly aware of it.

c. Illumination is the stage which has been referred to as the "Aha Phenomenon!" The creator suddenly sees the idea or solution to the problem.

d. Verification is the stage of testing the idea.

Name the stages of the creative process that you think Isaac Newton experienced when he was in the following situations:

During a severe storm, sixteen-year-old Isaac was asked to check the animals in the barn. Later he was found jumping from the fence, trying to find a way to measure the speed of wind.

While in a contemplative mood on the farm, he saw an apple fall to the ground, which led to the discovery of the law of gravitation.

When he devised integral calculus, he worked out the area of a hyperbola. He was so pleased with the accomplishment that he carried out one calculation to fifty-two figures.

Analyze and describe examples in your own life when you experienced the four stages of the creative process. Investigate the four stages of the creative process in the work and lives of creative people.

CREATIVE ENCOUNTER #4.........Space Exploration

By applying Newton's laws and advancing his inventions, scientists were enabled to peer farther and deeper into the universe. Write your creative story by completing the following open-ended sentences.

Space Exploration Cruise

I stepped into my zipansit to be transported for a relaxing exploration cruise. Swiftly I traveled across the country to the breathtaking view of the Rocky Mountains and in the next few moments back to my home. As I was leisurely enjoying the sunrise, my zipansit tipped upside down, and fortunately my zelephone flipped on. Desperately I punched my zelephone to notify my rescue computer. As I entered a time machine, I viewed my

hometown in the years 1800, 1900, and 2000. When I punched the future, it showed ___

_____ .

I guided the instruments of my zipansit for the expedition into space to join the seven

other spaceships. I was a captain, and the responsibilities of my job were _____

_____ .

As I gazed into space, I viewed _____

_____ .

Bright lights were flashing in my zipansit, which signaled that danger was lurking

ahead. I immediately contacted planet Earth. My message was _____

_____ .

I checked my supplies and survival kit. Some of my supplies on this journey were _____

_____ .

The flashing lights ceased, and I was safely resting in my cabin. The experience of

weightlessness was like _____

_____ .

Our scientists were searching for information about the complex topics of light, gravity,

and computer technology. Some of their most recent discoveries were _____

_____ .

The adventurous sights of the world of the future surrounded us. I slowly opened the door and breathed a sigh of relief as I stepped out of my zipansit.

For further space exploration:
Create your own Tomorrowland. Choose whether you would like the setting to be on Earth or in space. Dramatize an event there. On the back of this sheet, draw an illustration of your Tomorrowland and sketch a map of your space expedition. Draw a picture of your spaceship and the house you will live in.

INDEPENDENT PROJECTS—NEWTON

1. Study Newton's laws. Conduct science experiments demonstrating Newton's discoveries.
2. Compare the lives of Isaac Newton and Albert Einstein.
3. Sketch the size, shape, and position of the moon for one month.
4. Conduct solar power experiments. Make a sundial or a solar cooker.
5. Make a diagram of a telescope. Explain the difference between reflecting and refracting telescopes. Investigate the characteristics of various lenses and prisms.
6. Develop your spatial ability by experimenting with activities using tangrams, geoboards, tetrahedrons, and geometric shapes.
7. List objects that you would leave in a time box that would tell future generations what life was like at this time.
8. Write a scenario about space and the future.
9. Research the moon, Halley's comet, gravity, or a topic on stars, planets, or aerodynamics.
10. Organize a debate about the advantages and disadvantages of the space program.
11. Visit a planetarium or an observatory.
12. Identify career opportunities in mathematics, physics, science, astronomy, and computer technology.

RESOURCE BOOKS—NEWTON

Bergamini, David. *Mathematics.* New York: Time, Inc., for the Life Science Library, 1972.

Bixby, William. *The Universe of Galileo and Newton.* New York: American Heritage Publishing Co., Inc., 1964.

Branley, Franklyn M. *Experiments in the Principles of Space Travel.* rev. ed. New York: Thomas Y. Crowell Co., 1973.

Brown, Bob. *Science Treasures: Let's Repeat the Great Experiments.* New York: Fleet Press Corporation, 1968.

Greenleaf, Peter. *Experiments in Space Science.* New York: Arco Publishing, Inc., 1981.

Knight, David C., ed. *American Astronauts and Spacecraft: A Pictorial History from Project Mercury Through the Skylab Manned Missions.* New York: Franklin Watts, Inc., 1975.

Land, Barbara. *The Telescope Makers from Galileo to the Space Age.* New York: Thomas Y. Crowell Co., 1968.

Lerner, Aaron B. *Einstein & Newton: A Comparison of the Two Greatest Scientists.* Minneapolis: Lerner Publications Co., 1973.

Pickering, James S. *Famous Astronomers.* New York: Dodd, Mead & Co., 1968.

Schultz, Pearle and Harry. *Isaac Newton: Scientific Genius.* Champaign, Illinois: Garrard Publishing Co., 1972.

Sootin, Harry. *Isaac Newton.* New York: Julian Messner, Inc., 1955.

Tannenbaum, Beulah, and Myra Stillman. *Isaac Newton: Pioneer of Space Mathematics.* New York: Whittlesey House, 1959.

JONI EARECKSON TADA

"I am an artist. I creatively and expressively release what is inside. In my case that may mean writing books or speaking. It may mean spending hours in front of an easel portraying God's beauty in nature. It has even meant a bit of drama as I shared my life on film. Artists in the truest sense can always, with timing and balance, express creativity in any number of ways.

"My days are filled with meaningful and productive work. I'm surrounded by good friends and loved ones. And in spite of my disability, I live an independent life...I even drive my own van.

"I have entered a whole new world of thinking and independence. It is an exciting and encouraging time for me but I believe it will also open doors for other handicapped people across the country."

BIOGRAPHICAL SKETCH

On July 30, 1967, a lovely seventeen-year-old girl stepped to the edge of a floating dock and dived into the shallow water of the Chesapeake Bay. Joni felt her head strike something hard and unyielding, and she heard a loud electric buzzing, an unexplainable inner sensation. Her broken neck instantly sentenced Joni to a wheelchair for life, paralyzed from her shoulders down. In seconds her entire life was changed from a life of vivaciousness and independence to an existence of total helplessness and dependence. As an energetic teen-ager, her hopes and dreams were crushed. Just living became an ordeal, and she struggled against depression, bitterness, and confusion.

To occupy her long, lonely hours while recuperating, Joni began developing an artistic talent by using her mouth to guide her pen. An interview with Barbara Walters on NBC-TV's *Today Show* in 1974 sparked great interest nationally. Word of her artistic ability spread. Soon her artistic creations were reprinted on note cards, stationery and plaques.

Despite the fact that Joni is a quadriplegic, she refuses to let her handicap keep her from being all she can be. She produces award-winning paintings, writes books, portrays her own role in films, records best-selling albums, speaks, and directs an organization. On July 3, 1982, Joni married Ken Tada, a high school history and physical education teacher, who also works with Special Olympics. They hope that their marriage will serve as an encouragement to other handicapped people.

As a result of her books and films, Joni received thousands of letters from people who identified with her struggles. In 1979 Joni founded Joni and Friends in Woodland Hills, California. This nonprofit organization is designed to develop educational training materials and programs to help churches, community service organizations and businesses become aware and meet the needs of disabled people. A radio program entitled *Joni and Friends* also provides assistance and encouragement to those people suffering from handicaps and other problems. *Let's Be Friends*, a thirty-minute film, highlights Ken and Joni discussing her disability with elementary children. In 1983 Ken and Joni toured Europe to speak to large groups of disabled people. They eagerly face a future of continued service to those who suffer.

CREATIVE ENCOUNTER #1.........A Class Discussion

"There was an unusually strong bond of love which tied us together as a family. Mom was a source of that strength. She, too, loved the outdoors and athletic competition and shared Dad's interests. In fact, it was she who taught us girls to play tennis. Swimming and hiking were also things we did as a family. Mom, with her strong character and loving personality, worked as hard as Daddy to see that we had a happy home."

Joni grew up in a family that placed great value on living an active life and participating in sports. Imagine her feelings when she realized that she could never again go hiking or swimming. Do you think she had to readjust her value system? In what ways? Imagine how you would feel if you could never again walk, run, ride a bike, or hold a pencil.

CREATIVE ENCOUNTER #2.........A Creative Composition

"All of us have different kinds of handicaps and we struggle with different kinds of problems. Although having the same problem as someone else helps us to feel with them, we can still be of immense encouragement to those who suffer more than we do.

"Suffering sets the stage on which good qualities can perform. If we never had to face fear, we would know nothing about courage. If we never had to weep, we would never know what it was like to have a friend wipe tears from our eyes."

When tragedy strikes a person's life, is he/she a helpless victim? Does he/she have choices? Do you think that in some cases a person "chooses" to be a helpless victim rather than to overcome or to be in control of his situation? What choice did Joni make? How is this choice reflected in the things she says and does? Do you think a person's attitude can determine whether or not he can successfully cope with life's problems? Express your thoughts and ideas in a composition.

CREATIVE ENCOUNTER #3.........Group Discussion

"All during my childhood Daddy encouraged me to draw. He's a self-taught artist. My experiences charged me with creative energy and a maturity I didn't have before, and my art had a new quality and professionalism.

"For the first time, I threw myself fully into my artwork. I sketched pictures of things that had beauty rather than things that expressed emotions or hurts I'd experienced. It was a positive collection, with hope reflected in the drawings of animals, scenes, and people. As a result, people accepted them. They were attracted to sketches of youngsters, mountains, flowers, and forest animals because of the common beauty such subjects expressed."

Why do you think Joni chose to draw positive (happy) things rather than negative (sad) things? What does this tell you about her attitude? When you are feeling sad or discouraged, does it help to focus on the positives in your life rather than dwelling on your problems?

CREATIVE ENCOUNTER #4.........Class Project

"After the accident, Mom was the one who took charge at the hospital. She stayed there around the clock the first four days, catching short naps on a sofa in the lounge. She did not leave until she was absolutely certain I was out of danger.

"When Mom and Dad came, I always asked to be flipped if I was facing the floor. While they joked and got down on the floor if I was face down, I was deeply hurt that they had to go through the indignity of crawling around on the floor in order to visit with me."

Handicapped people need to feel worthwhile and loved. Instead, they often feel worthless and isolated. Relating in a positive way to a handicapped person can help to relieve the negative feelings he/she often experiences. The following are some suggestions for positive ways to relate to the handicapped:

—Don't stare or avoid a handicapped person. Instead, greet him/her with a warm smile or friendly conversation.

—Allow a handicapped person to be independent and to do things for himself. Suggest that he let you know if he needs your help. If you don't understand him, ask him to repeat himself.

Think of other positive ways of relating to someone who is handicapped. Make a poster of "Do's and Don't's."

CREATIVE ENCOUNTER #5.........Creative Drama

"Diana tried another experiment in role playing. This time, I saw my situation as others do. She sat in the chair, and I was on the sofa. 'Joni, I'd like a glass of water,' Diana said, pretending to be helpless."

Joni learned more about herself and others by role playing. Pretending to be another person sometimes helps us to better understand that person's feelings. Role play the following situation: Your friend is in a wheelchair. He shares his hurt feelings and frustration that he cannot play baseball. You are sympathetic and try to comfort your friend. Encourage him to discover and use other talents. Create other similar situations to role play.

CREATIVE ENCOUNTER #6.........Creative Interview

"Young people have always been drawn to my wheelchair and have responded with warmth and empathy to my disability."

If you were to meet Joni Eareckson Tada today, what would you say? Imagine that you are going to interview her. Make up a list of questions for your interview.

NAME _____

"Handicapped people have to get used to little tasks becoming big chores."

Joni has to wear a surgical support garment and a tight corset to aid her as she breathes. In order for Joni to sing the sustained notes on her record album, she needed a great deal of breath. So not only did she have to wear a corset, but she wore a seat belt. If she had to sing any high notes or long sustained notes, she tightened the seat belt to get more breath.

Think of all the things you do everyday that you take for granted (for example, walking up the steps to your school, taking a drink from the water fountain, dribbling a basketball, etc.). Now imagine that you are confined to a wheelchair and cannot use your arms or legs. Identify ten things that you can no longer do and try to decide which of these things would be most difficult and frustrating to give up and which things would be least difficult to give up. List these ten things below, ranking them in order from 1 to 10 with #1 being the most difficult thing to give up. To the right of these items, list ten things that you can still do.

Ten things I can no longer do:

1. _____
2. _____
3. _____
4. _____
5. _____
6. _____
7. _____
8. _____
9. _____
10. _____

Ten things that I can still do:

1. _____
2. _____
3. _____
4. _____
5. _____
6. _____
7. _____
8. _____
9. _____
10. _____

Below are four boxes. In the first box, print the letter *A*. In the second box, again print the letter *A*, but use your other hand. Choose a different letter and repeat the activity in the third and fourth boxes.

What are some of your thoughts and feelings about this experience?

NAME _____

Accompanying this section are some of Joni's drawings. Study these drawings carefully. In the space below, try sketching something of your own choosing—an animal, person, or scene. You might want to use Arthur Zaidenberg's books as references. (Don't worry if you're not "artistic"—just do the best you can!)

Now try sketching the same thing using only your teeth to steady the pen.

On the back of this work sheet, jot down some of your thoughts and feelings about this experience.

Kittens: © 1978 Joni
Deer: © 1976 Joni
Dog: © 1976 Joni

Joni Eareckson Tada's illustrations on this page and on page 101 can be used to add direction and focus to many of the Creative Encounters and Independent Projects suggested in this section.

Horse: ©1976 Joni

1. Joni Eareckson Tada turned her suffering and disability into an asset. Think of others who have overcome tragic situations. Choose one of these people and write a report on him/her. Explain how problems and suffering can build character and positively influence others.
2. "Listen" to a rainbow. Imagine that you must describe a rainbow to a person who cannot see. Be creative. Remember, you must help him "see" with his ears.
3. Create a self-portrait. Emphasize your positive qualities. Collect pictures that represent yourself, your hobbies, interests, and philosophy of life.
4. Imagine that you are a very young child. Look at your surroundings from the viewpoint of a child. Now draw or paint a picture in a childlike way.
5. Express your ideas about happiness in a collage. Collect photographs and magazine and newspaper clippings that reflect happy times.
6. Read *Kathy*, a true story about a girl whose life was shattered by a car accident. Compare her experiences with those of Joni.
7. Research recent technological advances that have made life easier for the handicapped. Include advances in several areas, such as hearing impairments, visual impairments, and learning disabilities.
8. Find ways in which you can help the handicapped in your community. Contact rehabilitation centers, special classes, etc., and ask how you can help. Or, if possible, offer your help to a family who has a handicapped child.

RESOURCE BOOKS—TADA

Ames, Lee J. *Draw 50 Dogs*. Garden City, New York: Doubleday & Co., Inc., 1981.

Batterberry, Ariane Ruskin, and Michael Batterberry. *The Pantheon Story of American Art for Young People*. New York: Pantheon Books, 1976.

Berger, Gilda. *Physical Disabilities*. New York: Franklin Watts, Inc., 1979.

Dunbar, Robert E. *Mental Retardation*. New York: Franklin Watts, 1978.

Eareckson, Joni, and Joe Musser. *Joni*. Grand Rapids, Michigan: Zondervan Publishing House, 1976.

Eareckson, Joni, and Steve Estes. *A Step Further*. Grand Rapids, Michigan: Zondervan Publishing House, 1978.

Kamien, Janet. *What If You Couldn't . . .? A Book About Special Needs*. New York: Charles Scribner's Sons, 1979.

Miller, Barbara, and Charles Paul Conn. *Kathy*. Old Tappan, New Jersey: Fleming H. Revell Co., 1980.

Miller, Barbara, and Kathy Miller. *We're Gonna Win*. Old Tappan, New Jersey: Fleming H. Revell Co., 1983.

Newman, Gene. *All God's Children*. Woodlands Hills, California: Joni and Friends, 1981.

Weiss, Malcolm E. *Blindness*. New York: Franklin Watts, Inc., 1980.

Wolf, Bernard. *Connie's New Eyes*. New York: J.B. Lippincott Co., 1976.

Wolf, Bernard. *Don't Feel Sorry for Paul*. New York: J.B. Lippincott Co., 1974.

Zaidenberg, Arthur. *Drawing All Animals*. Cleveland, Ohio: The World Publishing Co., 1967.

Zaidenberg, Arthur. *How to Draw Flowers, Fruit and Vegetables*. New York: Abelard-Schuman, 1964.

CORRIE TEN BOOM

"This was the beginning of my rich inheritance. When I remember my family life, I realize that my parents and my aunts had truly mastered the art of living. They enjoyed life and they loved children.

"In our hearts we must have stored some of the memory of laughter to be brought out in later years, when the sounds of happy voices were scarce in our beloved land.

"Children need the wisdom of their elders; the aging need the encouragement of a child's exuberance. Wisdom and exuberance lived side by side in the Beje, a house filled with varied personalities of the old and the young.

"Today I know that memories are the key not to the past, but to the future. I know that the experiences of our lives, when we let God use them, become the mysterious and perfect preparation for the work He will give us to do."

BIOGRAPHICAL SKETCH

For the first fifty years of her life, Cornelia Arnolda Johanna ten Boom lived peacefully with her family above the watch shop in Haarlem, Holland. Corrie learned watchmaking, and she became Holland's first licensed female watchmaker. This opened the door for other women to enter that field. Although the family did not gain great material wealth, they enjoyed a rich quality of life. The Beje, the name of the ten Boom home, was a refuge for "adopted" ten Booms: abandoned foster children, displaced refugees, and hunted Jews.

During World War II the Nazis turned Holland into a place of terror and destruction. The ten Booms were imprisoned for being leaders in the Dutch Underground and hiding Jewish refugees in a specially built room in their home. In solitary confinement Corrie faced the hopeless situation of being in a dirty and desolate prison where she suffered from malnutrition and from the stress of not knowing about her family and friends.

After the agonizing separation from her family, Corrie was reunited with her sister Betsie, and they were transported by train to Ravensbruck, a dreaded concentration camp in Germany. Betsie died at Ravensbruck, but Corrie was later released. In 1959 Corrie was part of a group which revisited Ravensbruck to honor Betsie and the ninety-six thousand other women who died there. While she was there, Corrie discovered that her own release had been a result of a clerical "error." One week later all women her age were sent to the gas chambers.

In her latter years Corrie traveled around the world captivating audiences with her inspiring story. She spoke four or five times a day and counseled people in between sessions. She visited embassies, native villages, royal courts, and prisons using any mode of transportation available, including elephants and rickshaws.

Her books have sold millions, and many people have seen the thrilling account of her wartime experiences in the film *The Hiding Place*. Corrie ten Boom has been called "one of the towering women of our time," and she has received many accolades. Countless lives that she has touched have been motivated and encouraged by her example.

CREATIVE ENCOUNTER #1.........Past, Present, and Future

*"I was watching the actors during the filming of **The Hiding Place.** The women who came out of the prison gate looked tired and cold. Then I saw the woman who was playing Corrie ten Boom. There I was, sitting and looking at my own story! Suddenly it was too much. I could not keep my tears back any longer. But through that a deep wound was healed. I knew why I had had that time of suffering. I learned a lesson that I could share with many people the world over."*

1. How would you react while watching the story of your life unfold in living color?

   _____

   _____

2. If you could paint a picture of your past, present, and future, what would be the

   colors? _____

   Why? _____

   _____

3. If you could attend any event in the past, present, or future, what would this event

   be? _____

4. Describe your early childhood memories. _____

   _____

   _____

   _____

5. Draw your family, interests, and hobbies in an illustration to represent your present life.

"Father had a special talent in directing our talks so that no one would feel left out. We loved to tell personal stories, but were taught to laugh at ourselves, not to make fun of others.

"In the camps and conferences, one of the biggest dangers was the gossip. We made a camp law and one of the articles was: 'If you must tell something negative about someone else, first tell ten positive qualities about him.'"

Sit in a circle. Take a few moments to think of compliments for your friends. Then sincerely compliment and give special words of encouragement to each person in your group.

Carole C. Carlson describes Corrie ten Boom in her biography: *"What a contrasting personality! Demanding, yet dependent. Brilliantly perceptive, yet curiously childlike."*

Brainstorm: Think of words that describe your friends.
Select the words to fit acrostic patterns for their names.
Write your acrostics in calligraphy. Display them on the bulletin board. Another idea for you is to create acrostics for gifts or cards.

CREATIVE ENCOUNTER #3.........A Class Project

"Then Holland surrendered. I walked in the street with Father, and everyone was talking to everyone else. In that moment there was a oneness which I had never seen before. We were together in the great suffering, humiliation, and defeat of our nation. Although my heart was aching with misery, there was encouragement that people could be so united."

Discuss other events throughout history that caused a special unity of the people in America and/or in other countries.

What are causes of disunity in a country?

Compare and contrast life in a free country with life in a country under a dictatorship. Refer to Corrie ten Boom's experiences before and after the invasion by the Nazis.

Write a research paper about your comparisons.

CREATIVE ENCOUNTER #4.........Leadership Qualities

Corrie ten Boom was a leader who served other people. She was a disciplined worker with high expectations; she would take risks. She had a keen sense of humor.

Brainstorm: Develop a list of characteristics of a leader.

Discuss the characteristics of the creative people in this book.

How are you applying and using these characteristics and qualities in your own life?

How are these people influencing your life?

Give a speech about how these people have influenced your life.

CREATIVE ENCOUNTER #5.........Meeting Challenges

In her eighty-fifth year, Corrie moved into a beautiful home in California, and she was involved in writing six books, making five films, and counseling. Continuing to set goals and meet challenges, she gave hope to those who feared growing old. By watching video tapes of her talks, she tried to improve herself. Corrie would critique her delivery and methods and would ask others to do the same.

Imagine that you are faced with the job of setting bigger goals and doing things better than you are now doing them.

Continue your current patterns, but try stepping up your activities. This approach offers new and challenging adventures.

State your goals. List the steps you will take to accomplish bigger and better goals.

_____

_____

_____

_____

CREATIVE ENCOUNTER #6..........Setting Goals

"We were always challenged to do our best. When Papa took a watch apart and put it back together again, it was a task he performed without regard to the owner's social status or wealth."

Write a journal or keep a chart of your goals and continued achievements.

AREA OF LIFE	GOALS	OBSTACLES	SOLUTIONS	REWARDS
School	Increase my reading	Not enough time	Set aside time	A more creative, interesting person
Friends				
Family				
Study Habits				
Jobs				
Physical Fitness				
Sports				
Music				
Hobbies				
Personal Habits				
Helping Others				
Finances				

INDEPENDENT PROJECTS—
TEN BOOM

1. Display baby pictures of your class on a bulletin board entitled "Our Past." Guess the names of the babies.
2. Invite resource people to speak about their goals and careers. Interview the people and ask them about the preparation that was needed to achieve their goals.
3. Research the education and preparation for job opportunities. Make a learning center about a variety of careers. Teach a lesson about career education.
4. Place students' school pictures on a bulletin board. Include illustrations about current activities. Entitle the bulletin board "Our Present."
5. Research the historical facts, causes, and effects of World War II and other wars.
6. Read about the life of Anne Frank.
7. Draw a diagram of the Beje, the ten Boom home.
8. Read about the clubs organized by Corrie. Organize a club and make up the rules. Explain why others should join your club. If you are a member of a club, give a presentation about it.
9. Visualize yourself ten, twenty, or more years from now. What would you like to do in the future? What are your main goals in life? Display illustrations of future goals and plans on a bulletin board entitled "Our Future."

RESOURCE BOOKS—TEN BOOM

Brown, Joan Winmill. *Corrie: The Lives She's Touched.* Old Tappan, New Jersey: Fleming H. Revell Co., 1979.

Carlson, Carole C. *Corrie ten Boom: Her Life, Her Faith.* Old Tappan, New Jersey: Fleming H. Revell Co., 1983.

Stamps, Ellen de Kroon. *My Years with Corrie.* Old Tappan, New Jersey: Fleming H. Revell Co., 1978.

ten Boom, Corrie. *Clippings from My Notebook.* Nashville, Tennessee: Thomas Nelson, Inc., Publishers, 1982.

ten Boom, Corrie. *Corrie's Christmas Memories.* Old Tappan, New Jersey: Fleming H. Revell Co., 1976.

ten Boom, Corrie. *Corrie ten Boom's Prison Letters.* Old Tappan, New Jersey: Fleming H. Revell Co., 1975.

ten Boom, Corrie. *Father ten Boom: God's Man.* Old Tappan, New Jersey: Fleming H. Revell Co., 1973.

ten Boom, Corrie, and Carole C. Carlson. *In My Father's House: The Years Before "The Hiding Place."* Old Tappan, New Jersey: Fleming H. Revell Co., 1976.

ten Boom, Corrie, John Sherrill, and Elizabeth Sherrill. *The Hiding Place.* Old Tappan, New Jersey: Fleming H. Revell Co., 1971.

Watson, Jean. *The Watchmaker's Daughter.* Old Tappan, New Jersey: Fleming H. Revell Co., 1983.

JIM THORPE

"Two or three weeks will put anyone in perfect condition if he is willing to work out properly. My own system at Carlisle was to go out on a few warm days, jog and exercise for two or three hours in the morning under a hot sun in heavy sweat clothes, come in and take a nap, and then go back in the afternoon and repeat the performance. During this period I did not eat very much food and drank practically no water. To stay right, all you have to do is get plenty of rest and know what you are going to do before you do it, and then act."

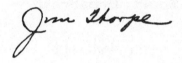

BIOGRAPHICAL SKETCH

James Francis Thorpe had the Indian name Wa-Tho-Huck, which means Bright Path. Jim came from a family of champions, and early in his life he dedicated himself to being one, too. By his seventh birthday, he had gone on many fishing and hunting trips. Shortly after his tenth birthday, he had killed his first deer with a rifle shot, and he tried breaking a colt.

Jim and his twin brother Charlie attended the Sac and Fox reservation school, which was twenty-three miles from the ranch. After his twin's death, Jim ran away from school and returned home. Immediately, his father walked him back to school. After his father left, Jim ran cross-country over a shorter, rougher route. When his father arrived home, his son was waiting for him. Determined that his son should go to school, his father sent him to Haskell Institute, a government school for Indians. When Jim heard that his father was wounded in a hunting accident, Jim journeyed on foot for two weeks to their ranch, a distance of about 300 miles.

In 1912 at Stockholm Jim Thorpe became the only athlete to win both the Olympic pentathlon and decathlon events. As he presented Jim Thorpe the magnificent trophies, the King of Sweden said, *"Sir, you are the greatest athlete in the world."* Because Jim had been paid a few dollars to play semiprofessional baseball, the Olympic medals and trophies were taken away from him, and his records were erased. However, the Olympic medals have since been returned to his family.

Jim Thorpe is the only athlete to win gold medals in track and field, win All-American honors in college football, play big-time professional football, and play major-league baseball. In 1920, he was elected the first president of the American Professional Football Association. At the 1932 Olympic Games in California, he shared the Presidential box with Vice-President Charles Curtis, and the crowd gave Jim Thorpe a standing ovation. He was one of the first members admitted to the Football Hall of Fame. In 1950, Jim Thorpe was voted the greatest football player and the greatest male athlete of the first half of the twentieth century.

CREATIVE ENCOUNTER #1.........Creative Drama

The Thorpe twins roamed the prairies, learned how to catch fish with the spears of their ancestors, raced, and played vigorous games. *"Many a time in these games I had to swim rivers, climb barns, jump off roofs, wade streams, and ride horses."*

During Jim's childhood, ranch work and games of endurance were splendid training for the coordination and precision that he needed later in life. Jim Thorpe excelled in any sport that he tried: football, track, baseball, archery, swimming, hockey, shooting, canoeing, basketball, tennis, lacrosse, handball, gymnastics, and horseback riding.

1. Pantomime your favorite sport or athlete.
2. Sit in a circle. Pass an imaginary football to the person next to you. That person changes the football to something else and passes it on. Each person must guess what the object is when it is passed to him/her. Continue passing a variety of imaginary objects around the circle.

CREATIVE ENCOUNTER #2.........A Sports Broadcast

The following are some sports facts about Jim Thorpe:

Jim Thorpe and six Indians from Carlisle School competed against Lafayette's unbeaten team of forty-eight men in a track meet. Carlisle won, 71-41.

The future General and President "Ike" Eisenhower of West Point played against the great Indian in football. Carlisle won, 27-6.

When the United States Olympic team sailed to Stockholm, the athletes jogged, lifted weights, and did calisthenics. Jim Thorpe measured off distances on the ship's deck, resumed his mental workouts, and dozed on a deck chair. While the athletes limbered up in Stockholm, he relaxed in a hammock. Jim needed only a short period to work himself into top shape, and then he could stay in excellent condition by competing, concentrating, and relaxing.

Before the competition at the Olympics, he could not find his favorite spikes so he competed in borrowed track shoes.

Discuss other events, highlights, and amazing facts about athletes in the sports world.

If you could interview Jim Thorpe and other athletes, what would you discuss?

Become an athlete of the past or present. Plan a sports broadcast and have your classmates interview you.

CREATIVE ENCOUNTER #3.........Sports Events

Jim Thorpe wrote a letter to the Amateur Athletic Union about the issue of returning his Olympic medals.

"I did not play for the money there was in it, but because I like to play ball. I was not very wise to the ways of the world. I hope I will be partly excused by the fact that I was an Indian school boy and did not know that I was doing wrong."

Read about the sports events of the Olympics.

Write a paper comparing and contrasting the past rules, strategies, equipment, and events of sports to those of the present sports world.

CREATIVE ENCOUNTER #4 ....Learning from Problems

Early in his life, Jim Thorpe faced the deaths of his twin brother, his mother and father. Later his first son died. He also faced the disappointment of giving up his Olympic medals.

Coach Warner recognized the prowess, the versatility, and the vigor of Jim Thorpe and helped him to develop into an Olympic champion. What people in your life believe in you and encourage you?

In contrast, Coach McGraw of the New York Giants made Jim sit on the bench a lot. The "Little Napoleon" of baseball seemed more interested in breaking Jim's spirit than in developing his potential.

Throughout your life you may meet people who discourage and criticize you and cause frustration. Joyce Landorf, an author and speaker, states in her book *Irregular People* that these people cannot see your talents, skills, or successes in your field of endeavor. However, "irregular people," stress, and trials can help build your character, provide new insight, and help you to understand other people's problems.

What are you learning from your problems?

How have your problems helped you to identify with others?

How have you overcome discouraging remarks and circumstances?

What new insight have you gained?

How have these trying circumstances changed your attitude and built your character?

Find new, innovative ways to cope with your problems.

Try keeping a personal diary of your progress and goals.

CREATIVE ENCOUNTER #5..........A Class Project

Plan a Sports Day. Choose a topic from the following list to research in the world of sports:

Game strategies and rules

The lives of athletes

Specific sporting events

How sports and competition can build character

Characteristics of athletes

Then design a poster with some rules for good sportsmanship.

Display your trophies and awards in sports.

Share your experiences in sports events.

Present a commercial to convince others that exercise is important to their health. Wear your jogging suit.

Present your research during a sports broadcast or in a panel discussion.

Plan competitive sports, awards, and physical exercise for Sports Day.

CREATIVE ENCOUNTER #6..........Admirable Qualities

Jim was proud of his father, a champion wrestler, jumper, and swimmer. He wanted to grow up to be a champion like his father. Sometimes Jim and his father would walk twenty or thirty miles a day on their hunting trips.

"Once when we didn't have enough horses to carry our kill, my father slung a buck deer over each shoulder and carried them twenty miles to our home. I have never known a man with such energy. He could walk, ride, and run for days without ever showing the least sign of fatigue."

Jim Thorpe often spoke of his admiration for Chief Black Hawk, his ancestor, who was the greatest warrior of the Sac and Fox tribe. Jim Thorpe said, *"I am no more proud of my career as an athlete than I am of the fact that I am a direct descendant of the noble warrior."*

1. What people do you admire?

   _____

   _____

2. What qualities and achievements do you admire about these people?

   _____

   _____

3. What accomplishments and honors have you attained?

   _____

   _____

4. What award or words of praise or recognition would mean a lot to you?

   _____

5. Express your thoughts in creative writing about admirable qualities and greatness. Your creative writing could include the qualities of an athlete, who has received public recognition, or qualities of a mother, who may not receive any public recognition for her care of a home and children.

_____

_____

_____

_____

_____

CREATIVE ENCOUNTER #7..........Creating a Game

Make up a new game. Your new game could be a mental game, an outdoor game, a sports event in the Olympics, or a game that could be played in the future.

Design and describe the rules, strategies, equipment, and clothing used for your game.

Draw pictures of equipment, clothing, positioning, etc., below.

INDEPENDENT PROJECTS—THORPE

1. Organize games and activities for younger children.
2. Keep a scrapbook of sports events and your own sports achievements.
3. Begin your own daily exercise program. Keep a chart of your progress.
4. Become a coach. Explain the rules and strategies of a game.
5. Brainstorm. List all the games that you can think of that use balls.
6. Make a mural about Indian topics: games, culture, customs, crafts, music, clothing, history, language, tools, or family life.
7. Write an essay from the point of view of a baseball, basketball, volleyball, football, tennis racket, ice skate, canoe, water ski, or snow ski.
8. Imagine yourself as a sports hero. Write about your training, goals, and achievements. Plan a skit about your life as a sports hero.
9. Design an award or trophy you would like to receive if you were a sports hero.
10. Research the lives and training routines of famous athletes, such as Glenn Cunningham and Roy Campanella, who suffered from physical injuries. Write an inspirational essay of tribute to these sports heroes.
11. Read about sports for the handicapped. Make a chart describing and illustrating these opportunities for the handicapped.
12. Make up analogies relating sports to experiences in life. Some examples are the following: How is life like running a race?
    How is learning to control what we say like learning to ski?
    How is learning to face problems like climbing mountains?

RESOURCE BOOKS—THORPE

Allen, Anne. *Sports for the Handicapped.* New York: Walker and Co., 1981.

Brondfield, Jerry. *Great Moments in American Sports.* New York: Random House, Inc., 1974.

Hollander, Zander, comp. and ed. *Great American Athletes of the 20th Century.* New York: Random House, Inc., 1966.

Killanin, Lord, and John Rodda, eds. *The Olympic Games 1980.* New York: Macmillan Publishing Co., Inc., 1979.

Landorf, Joyce. *Irregular People.* Waco, Texas: Word, Inc., 1982.

Libby, Bill. *Stars of the Olympics.* New York: Hawthorn Books, Inc., 1975.

Reising, Robert. *Jim Thorpe.* Minneapolis: Dillon Press, Inc., 1974.

Schaap, Dick. *An Illustrated History of the Olympics.* 3rd ed., enl. New York: Ballantine Books, 1976.

Schoor, Gene, and Henry Gilfond. *The Jim Thorpe Story: America's Greatest Athlete.* New York: Julian Messner, Inc., 1951.

Van Riper, Guernsey, Jr. *Jim Thorpe: Indian Athlete.* New York: The Bobbs-Merrill Co., Inc., 1961.

MARIA VON TRAPP

"And now—to make a long story short—I fell in love! For the first time in my life. I fell in love with those wonderful children. There they were—from age four to fourteen—two boys and five girls. I don't know how it happened, but in no time we were just one heart and one soul.

" 'And they lived happily ever after,' one could almost say as the years went by. We had two hobbies in our family. One was to hike together and the other was to sing together. Both would prove very important one day for the Trapp family.

"For twenty blissful years we had traveled the world together, bringing music to people and experiencing at every concert what a great peacemaker music is."

Maria von Trapp

BIOGRAPHICAL SKETCH

Maria von Trapp grew up in Austria. Her parents died, and she was left as an orphan at an early age. She had an unhappy childhood. During her teen years Maria was an avid reader and was interested in learning foreign languages. She enjoyed playing any kind of musical instrument, hiking and traveling.

Maria stood on the threshold of a new life when she came from the middle ages atmosphere of a convent into the elegant home of a baron. She was very happy living with Baron Georg von Trapp and his seven children, ages four to fourteen.

After Austria was invaded, the two parents with their nine children and the tenth child on the way left their home inconspicuously by going on a hiking trip in the mountains. Overnight they had become poor refugees. In her husband's rucksack was the scrapbook of valuable contracts. Their hobby was turned into a way of making their living. When the Trapp Family Singers went on their European concert tour into Austria, they met cousins and friends who had lost everything, and most of them had also lost their sons to Hitler.

People from around the world have sent letters to the Trapp family, expressing their appreciation for the message of *The Sound of Music*. This famous family established the Trapp Family Music Camp and the Trapp Family Austrian Relief Fund. The home of the Trapp family of *The Sound of Music* fame is located high on a hill in the Green Mountains of Vermont. The Trapp Family Lodge offers an ideal place for a vacation with inspiring mountain views.

Maria von Trapp is a mother, homemaker, musician, lecturer, writer, and world traveler. Love, faith, humor, drama, and victory are elements of her memorable story.

The Trapp Family Singers have traveled and performed across the United States. Their family found that America is still the land of unlimited opportunities. "It is up to you to see them," Maria states. "And we had also found out that this was the only way to become American, a part of this nation of pioneers: to be a pioneer yourself."

CREATIVE ENCOUNTER #1.........Music and Nature

"The people were used to seeing us come out of our house dressed for mountain climbing with big knapsacks on our backs and mountain boots, walking around our garden fence to the little station where the local trains stopped that took us into the Alps. The people were also used to hearing us sing together by the hour on summer evenings."

Sing and listen to the record of *The Sound of Music* by Rodgers and Hammerstein.

What are your "favorite things?"

Go on a musical nature hike in your imagination. Imagine the joy and inspiration of music in nature. Listen to the music of nature—the singing of birds, the rhythm of animals, the splashing of the waterfall, the whistling of the wind, and the whisper of the breeze. Listen to the chiming of bells, the music of laughter, and the music in the air. What sounds of music can you hear in nature? What beautiful sounds and sights of nature and animals do you enjoy?

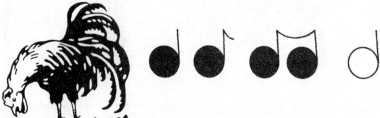

CREATIVE ENCOUNTER #2.........Rhythm Patterns

Discuss the names of notes, signatures of music, rhythm, and other topics of music theory. Create rhythm patterns with names of trees, flowers, animals, birds, etc. Say or sing the following words in the indicated rhythm:

Sycamore ♩ ♪ ♩   Water lily ♩ ♪ ♩ ♪

Sassafras ♪ ♪ ♪   Daisy ♩ ♩

Tulip tree ♩ ♪ ♪   Sunflower ♩ ♪ ♪ ♪

Morning glory ♩ ♪ ♪ ♪   Calico kitten ♪ ♩ ♪ ♪ ♪ ♩ ♩

Create and then play or tap the rhythm of something, giving a clue as to its category. For example, tap the rhythm of the following flower: ♪ ♪ ♪

Ask your classmates to guess the name of the flower. (petunia)

Brainstorm: What are the rhythms of nature and animals? Dramatize the rhythmic movements of nature and animals. Create rhythm patterns of the gait of a horse and other rhythmic movements of nature and animals.

White-tailed deer ♩ ♪ ♩ ♪   Raindrops ♩ ♪ ♩ ♪

Create rhythm patterns for the sounds of animals.

Rooster cock-a-doodle-doo ♩ ♪ ♫ ♩ European cuckoo ♩ ♩

Make up a story or compose a song. Play your rhythm patterns with percussion instruments in your story or song.

CREATIVE ENCOUNTER #3..........Honor and Freedom

"Look Lorli. You must never, never, do you understand, never tell anything at school that you hear at home. We'll all be put in a concentration camp if you don't keep silent. Do you understand me?

"My husband did not allow the swastika around the house or the new greeting or the new anthem to ever be heard. The pressure mounted and our lives were threatened by the Nazis.

"So half a year passed, and then came the moment when my husband called the family together and said, 'Do we want to keep our material goods, our house, our estate, our friends—or do we want to keep our spiritual goods, our faith and honor? We cannot have both any longer.'

"Then he looked at his children and said, 'Listen, you can have money today and lose it tomorrow. The very same day you can start all over again, and that can happen more than once to you in your lifetime. But once you have lost your honor or your faith, then you are lost.' "

1. What changes occur when a dictatorship invades a free country? _____

   _____

   _____

2. How do these changes affect the freedom and lives of families at home, church, and

   school? _____

   _____

   _____

   _____

3. How do these changes affect the politics and economics of the country? _____

   _____

4. Develop newspaper headlines which might have been printed about the above event
   or other major historical events.

   _____

   _____

   _____

CREATIVE ENCOUNTER #4..........Appreciating Home

"One has to have lost a home oneself to understand and appreciate what the words mean: home sweet home."

1. What does *home* mean to you? _____
   _____
   _____

2. What does *our country* mean to you? _____
   _____
   _____

3. What does *freedom* mean to you? _____
   _____
   _____

4. What can you do in your lifetime to preserve our freedom? _____
   _____
   _____
   _____

5. If you became a leader in the United States government, what steps would you take to help our country? _____
   _____
   _____

6. Express why you are thankful for our land of liberty. _____
   _____
   _____

Express your thoughts about these topics in a composition or speech.
Entitle your project "I Am Proud to Be an American."

CREATIVE ENCOUNTER #5..........A Coat of Arms

"In their coat of arms, the Trapps had the words: 'Nec aspera terrent'—'Let nothing difficult frighten thee.' That seemed quite appropriate to have been used by us so far. We needed it through the perilous cruise across dangerous waters. When we acquired our new citizenship, we gave up our title and the coat of arms, and somehow 'Nec aspera terrent,' which had served very well, was not so necessary any more. A new word to live by from now on had been given us now: 'Cor unum'. The goal is that the world should be able to say: 'Look how they love one another. They are one heart and one soul.'"

1. What are at least three symbols that you think represent you? (Examples: a piano to represent your interest in music, a soccer ball to represent your interest in sports, a

   heart for your family, an American flag) _____

   _____

   _____

   _____

2. What is one value you would not budge from? _____

   _____

3. What is your life motto? _____

   _____

Include your symbols, value, and motto as you design your own coat of arms.

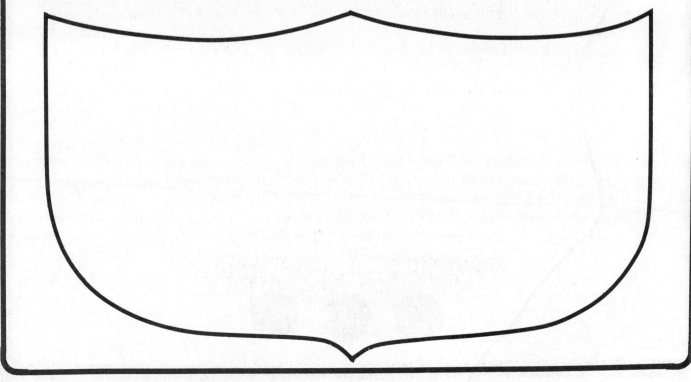

1. Go on a musical nature hike. Observe the music and rhythm in nature. Explore nature and sing while on the hike. Use what you find in nature for rhythm and movement.

2. Tape-record and study animal, bird, and nature sounds. Compare these sounds with music. If you were making a record about nature and animals, what sounds would you add?

3. Listen to *The Grand Canyon Suite* by Ferde Grofe. Dramatize the music to describe the beauty of nature. Become a part of nature—a rainbow, sunrise, sunset, waterfall, wind, cloudburst, or lightning.

4. Present dramatic episodes that tell about the backgrounds of American songs, such as "The Star-Spangled Banner," "The Battle Hymn of the Republic," or "America, the Beautiful."

5. Write a story, and include the titles of the songs of *The Sound of Music* and other well-known songs.

6. Think of phrases that follow "Happiness is . . . ." For example, "Happiness is a new puppy." Think of other phrases: "Family is . . . ." "A friend is . . . ." "America is . . . ." "Love is . . . ." "Funny is . . . ."

7. What motto would you like to hang in your home? Design a plaque, write your motto in calligraphy, and illustrate it. Give this plaque to your family, and hang it in your home.

8. Invite a resource person who knows a foreign language to your class. Study a foreign language.

RESOURCE BOOKS—VON TRAPP

Apel, Willi. *Harvard Dictionary of Music.* 2nd ed., rev. and enl. Cambridge: The Belknap Press of Harvard University Press, 1969.

Lindsay, Howard, and Russel Crouse. *The Sound of Music.* New York: Random House, 1960.

Lyons, John Henry. *Stories of Our American Patriotic Songs.* New York: The Vanguard Press, Inc., 1942.

Rublowsky, John. *Music in America.* New York: Crowell-Collier Press, 1967.

Scholes, Percy A. *The Oxford Junior Companion to Music.* London: Oxford University Press, 1954.

Sirmay, Albert, comp. *The Rodgers and Hammerstein Song Book.* New York: Simon and Schuster and Williamson Music, Inc., 1968.

Trapp, Maria Augusta. *The Story of the Trapp Family Singers.* New York: J.B. Lippincott Co., 1949.

Trapp, Maria Augusta, and Ruth T. Murdoch. *A Family on Wheels: Further Adventures of the Trapp Family Singers.* New York: J.B. Lippincott Co., 1959.

von Trapp, Maria. *Maria.* Carol Stream, IL.: Creation House, 1972.

LAURA INGALLS WILDER

"Across the years, the old home and its love called to me and memories of sweet words of counsel came flooding back. I realized that all my life the teachings of those early days have influenced me and the example set by my mother and father has been something I have tried to follow, with failures here and there, with rebellion at times, but always coming back to it as the compass needle to the star.

"The **Little House** Books are stories of long ago. Today our way of living and our schools are much different; so many things have made living and learning easier. But the real things haven't changed. It is still best to be honest and truthful; to make the most of what we have; to be happy with simple pleasures and to be cheerful and have courage when things go wrong. Great improvements in living have been made because every American has always been free to pursue his happiness, and so long as Americans are free they will continue to make our country ever more wonderful."

Laura Ingalls Wilder

BIOGRAPHICAL SKETCH

American ideals were conveyed in this pioneer home filled with love, hope, laughter, tears, responsibility, and adventure. Deep in the Big Woods in Wisconsin was a log cabin where Laura was born. Her family traveled by covered wagon through Kansas, Minnesota, and Dakota Territory.

Pa, Ma, Mary, Laura, Carrie, and Grace built their lives on sharing, respect, and concern for one another. Ma was a steadfast, ingenious woman, who was devoted with enduring love to her husband, to the establishment of their home, and to her children. In her fond memories, Half-Pint could see her pa playing the fiddle, singing, working in the fields, and walking with her family across the prairie to church in Walnut Grove.

Laura called herself a pioneer girl, who was filled with hopes and dreams that would one day be fulfilled. Laura helped Mary, her blind sister, with her lessons and earned money to send Mary to college. At fifteen, Laura began teaching school, and three years later she married Almanzo James Wilder. Their years together were filled with sunshine and shadow. Crops were destroyed, and their barn and haystacks burned. They both became sick, and their son died. When their house burned, only one thing from the kitchen was saved—a glass plate with the words: Give us this day our daily bread. With hard work and faith, they turned unpromising ridge land into a prosperous paradise that they called Rocky Ridge Farm. Laura often put aside her busy chores to reach and touch the beauty of nature.

Laura Elizabeth Ingalls Wilder had a delightful, cheerful personality and was filled with energy and determination. Laura's resourcefulness, strength, and charm are manifested in her books. Her series of books is filled with the scents, sounds, and sights of pioneer America and remembrances of school days, sleigh rides, and holiday celebrations.

CREATIVE ENCOUNTER #1..........A Creative Composition

"Life was not intended to be simply a round of work, no matter how interesting and important that work may be. A moment's pause to watch the glory of a sunrise or a sunset is soul-satisfying, while a bird's song will set the steps to music all day long.

"I believe we would be happier to have a personal revolution in our individual lives and go back to simpler living and more direct thinking. It is the simple things of life that make living worthwhile, the sweet fundamental things such as love and duty, work and rest and living close to nature.

"The true way to live is to enjoy every moment as it passes and surely it is in the everyday things around us that the beauty of life lies."

Comment about the above statements, which are a few thoughts that reflect Laura's philosophy of life. What is your philosophy of life?

Write a composition and state your philosophy of life.

CREATIVE ENCOUNTER #2..........American Pioneers

"Running through all the stories, like a golden thread, is the same thought of the values of life. They were courage, self-reliance, independence, integrity and helpfulness. Cheerfulness and humor were handmaids to courage," said Laura.

We step into the pages of the past with the series of *Little House* books. Imagine yourself living in these pioneer days. What would you like about living during this time in the United States? What are characteristics of early American pioneers?

Write a feature story about one of the following topics:

1. If you lived in the time of the early settlements of the United States, what practical suggestions would you have given to a family leaving to travel west?

2. Contrast the early American kitchen to the kitchen of today in relation to the following factors: cooking, refrigeration, and utensils.

CREATIVE ENCOUNTER #3..........Creative Drama

Compare the one-room school and activities of the past to the contemporary educational system.

Role play school day experiences during this time in American history. Refer to the books by Laura Ingalls Wilder.

CREATIVE ENCOUNTER #4.........Journey to "Little House"

Close your eyes. As your teacher reads this journey to the pioneer days, imagine yourself with Laura Ingalls Wilder.

Then draw illustrations and write about your favorite season of the year.

"Some morning early, when I can get away, I want you to come with me along the edge of the hill in the woodlot. When the shadows of the trees begin to come down the slope, as the sun rises you feel the turning of the earth. You feel the whole globe under your feet rolling into the sunlight.

"There is a purple haze over the hill tops and a hint of sadness in the sunshine, because of summer's departure: on the low ground down by the spring the walnuts are dropping from the trees and squirrels are busy hiding away their winter supply. Here and there the leaves are beginning to change color and a little, vagrant, autumn breeze goes wandering over the hills and down the valleys whispering to 'follow, follow,' until it is almost impossible to resist.

"We lay away the gleanings of our years in the edifice of our character, where nothing is ever lost. What have we stored away in this safe place during the season that is past? Is it something that will keep sound and pure and sweet or something that is faulty and not worth storing?"

_____

_____

_____

_____

_____

_____

_____

_____

_____

CREATIVE ENCOUNTER #5..........Exploring Etymology

"There is a fascination in writing. The use of words is of itself an interesting study. You will hardly believe the difference the use of one word rather than another will make until you begin to hunt for a word with just the right shade of meaning, just the right color for the picture you are painting with words. Had you thought that words have color?"

Etymology is the study of the history and development of words. The Greek word *etymon* = true meaning and *logos* = word, study.

For example, this is the etymology of the word *talent*. Matthew 25:14-30 tells the story of talents, which were amounts of money. The word is from the Greek word *talanton*, a sensitive scale for weighing valuables. Medieval talentum referred both to a unit of money and to mental aptitude. The word *alphabet* comes from the words *alpha* and *beta*, the first two letters of the Greek alphabet. The origin of *breakfast* comes from the Biblical concept of breaking the fast of the night, break + fast.

Imagine you are settlers in America. What would you have called a fish with whiskers? (a catfish)

Early settlers tended to attach simple, descriptive names to what they found in America. Settlers would apply words they already knew in a new way. They used onomatopoeia to name the katydid, whose three notes sounded like the name they gave it. A bird with a catlike cry was named catbird. A razorback is a slender, wild hog. A muskrat looks like a rat and has a musky odor. An apple or paring bee involved the preparation for making apple butter or dried apples.

Divide into two small groups. Using the following lists, each group prepares a set of questions similar to the question about catfish. One group presents questions to the other group, whose members attempt to think of the words actually used.

Words for Group I

catbird	sewing bee	muskrat
lightning bug	spelling bee	roasting ear
blue jay	quilting bee	katydid

Words for Group II

sweet potato	husking bee	popcorn
peanut	apple or paring bee	razorback
groundhog	threshing bee	foothills

CREATIVE ENCOUNTER #6.........A Creative Drawing

Explore the dictionary, and study the etymology of words. Find a word you would like to illustrate. Find the root/roots of this word. Make a creative drawing of the root/roots which shows the origin of your word. Share your ideas. The others can guess the words illustrated.
Here are examples.

Photograph: Greek phos = light and graphein = write.

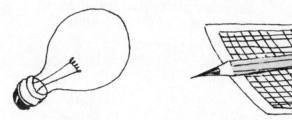

Microcosm: Greek mikros = little and kosmos = world, universe.

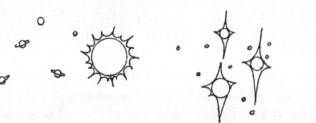

Zoology: Greek zoion = animal and logos = word, speech, study.

INDEPENDENT PROJECTS—WILDER

1. Research and write about your genealogy. Make a family tree.
2. Interview and tape-record your parents' and grandparents' childhood experiences.
3. Write and illustrate a book about your childhood.
4. Read about the pioneer families who settled in the United States.
5. Experiment with the recipes from *The Little House Cookbook*.
6. Research how education has changed throughout the years in the U.S.A. Make a chart describing and illustrating these changes.
7. Explore English words derived from Latin, Greek, and other languages.
8. List the names of places in your state and other states that originate from ancient history or the Bible.
9. Find the names of baby animals, such as joey and owlet.
10. Plan an old-fashioned spelling bee.

RESOURCE BOOKS—WILDER

Austin, Dorothea. *The Name Book*. Minneapolis: Bethany House Publishers, 1982.

Butterworth, Emma Macalik. *The Complete Book of Calligraphy*. New York: Lippincott & Crowell, Publishers, 1980.

Garson, Eugenia, comp. and ed. *The Laura Ingalls Wilder Songbook: Favorite Songs from the "Little House" Books*. New York: Harper & Row, Publishers, 1968.

Walker, Barbara M. *The Little House Cookbook: Frontier Foods from Laura Ingalls Wilder's Classic Stories*. New York: Harper & Row, Publishers, 1979.

Wilder, Laura Ingalls. *Farmer Boy*. New York: Harper & Row, Publishers, 1933.

Wilder, Laura Ingalls. *The First Four Years*. New York: Harper & Row, Publishers, 1971.

Wilder, Laura Ingalls. *Little House in the Big Woods*. New York: Harper & Row, Publishers, 1932.

Wilder, Laura Ingalls. *Little House on the Prairie*. New York: Harper & Row, Publishers, 1935.

Wilder, Laura Ingalls. *Little Town on the Prairie*. New York: Harper & Row, Publishers, 1941.

Wilder, Laura Ingalls. *The Long Winter*. New York: Harper & Row, Publishers, 1940.

Wilder, Laura Ingalls. *These Happy Golden Years*. New York: Harper & Row, Publishers, 1943.

Zochart, Donald. *Laura: The Life of Laura Ingalls Wilder*. Chicago: Henry Regnery Co., 1976.

ZIG ZIGLAR

"You can get everything in life you want, if you help enough other people get what they want. A sincere compliment is one of the most effective teaching and motivational methods in existence. You are the sum total of what goes into your mind. A positive attitude will have positive results because attitudes are contagious.

"You climb the highest by staying on the level. Opportunity for success lies in the person and not in the job. Ability is important. Dependability is critical.

"When you sow an action, you reap a habit; when you sow a habit, you reap a character; and when you sow a character, you reap a destiny. If you want to reach your goal, you must 'see the reaching' in your own mind before you actually arrive at your goal. Man was designed for accomplishment, engineered for success and endowed with the seeds of greatness."

Zig Ziglar

A BIOGRAPHICAL SKETCH

Motivational teacher Zig Ziglar has been called the Johnny Appleseed of the twentieth century because he crisscrosses America planting seeds of hope and teaching a plan of action so that people everywhere can grow to their full potential. Zig's enthusiasm, humor, and thirst for knowledge, combined with competent research assistants, keep his material and teaching techniques effective and timely. Widely acclaimed as America's superstar of salesmanship, Zig travels around the world inspiring audiences, training salesmen, and teaching the factors fundamental to personal success: a positive attitude and a healthy self-image. Anchoring his philosophy is the firm belief that the building blocks to genuine success are honesty, character, integrity, faith, loyalty, and love.

Zig is founder and chairman of the Zig Ziglar Corporation in Dallas, Texas. As a dynamic educator and trainer, he has produced several complete video series for business and education. He has made commercial movies and has created, produced, or participated in training programs for major national and international organizations.

The "I CAN" Course based on See You at the Top is being taught in kindergarten through adult education across America. See You at the Top, which has been translated into Braille and foreign languages, is serving as a textbook in numerous schools, churches, and correctional institutions. Teacher training and staff development workshops and seminars are held regularly across the United States. Marketed along with his books are audio cassette recordings ranging from single cassettes to his "Born to Win" series, which contains over twenty-five hours of personal development material.

Zig is rated by his peer group and by audiences everywhere as one of the best and most versatile speakers in America. Zig's concern for the welfare of his fellow man is evidenced by the time and training he provides to the underprivileged and criminal elements of society. Zig has been recognized in *The Congressional Record of the United States* for his work with youth in the drug war and for his activities in supporting America and the free enterprise system. Zig Ziglar has appeared on the platform with such outstanding Americans as Ronald Reagan, Paul Harvey, and Art Linkletter, as well as several United States senators, congressmen, and governors.

*"Several years ago, a balloon salesman was selling balloons on the streets of New York City. When business got a little slow, he would release a balloon. As it floated into the air, a fresh crowd of buyers would gather and his business would pick up for a few minutes. He alternated the colors, first releasing a white one, then a red one and later a yellow one. After a time, a little Negro boy tugged on his coat sleeve, looked the balloon salesman in the eye and asked a penetrating question. 'Mister, if you released a black balloon, would it go up?' The balloon salesman looked at the little boy and with compassion, wisdom and understanding said, 'Son, it's what's inside those balloons that make them go up.' The little boy was fortunate indeed to encounter a man who could see with more than just his eyes. With good eyes you can see to run or walk, work or play. The person who can see with his heart and his eyes can also reach out and touch the spirit within another human being and reveal the good that lies in him. Yes, the balloon salesman was 'right.' I'm also 'right' when I tell you, **it's what's inside you that will make you go up.**"* (See You at the Top)

1. Look up the word *compassion* in the dictionary. Write the definition.

   _____

   _____

2. Describe a situation when you have shown compassion and understanding for someone else.

   _____

   _____

   _____

   _____

3. What are some qualities that you think are necessary in order to climb the ladder to success? Write these qualities inside the balloons.

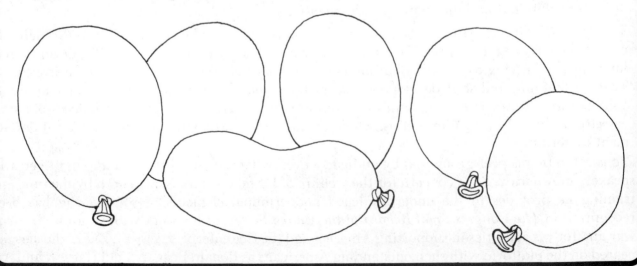

CREATIVE ENCOUNTER #2..........A Good Self-Image

1. Write about the importance of a good self-image and a positive attitude. List ways you plan to improve your self-image and attitude. For example, improve your self-image by reading biographies and listening to speakers and teachers who stress positive attitudes.

    1. _____
    2. _____
    3. _____
    4. _____
    5. _____
    6. _____
    7. _____
    8. _____
    9. _____
    10. _____

2. Make a victory list of your past successes. This list will remind you that you have succeeded in the past and that you can do it again. Continue to develop the list as time passes.

    1. _____
    2. _____
    3. _____
    4. _____
    5. _____
    6. _____
    7. _____
    8. _____
    9. _____
    10. _____

CREATIVE ENCOUNTER #3.........Key to Success

This page is based on *See You at the Top* by Zig Ziglar. Refer to the dictionary to help you with the definitions.

1. Name the six foundation stones you must build on to assure success.

   _____ _____

   _____ _____

   _____ _____

2. Define *ability*. _____

   _____

3. Define *dependability*. _____

4. Do you believe that a person who has character, trust, honesty, integrity, love and loyalty has a better chance for success? Yes ☐ No ☐

5. Think of someone you genuinely like and admire. How many of these qualities does this individual possess? _____

6. Define *character*. _____

7. Define *loyalty*. _____

8. The real opportunity for success lies within the person. How do you feel about this statement?

   _____

   _____

9. Had you considered the possibility that what you want is available if you develop the characteristics for success and climb the stairway to the top? Yes ☐ No ☐

10. How does the idea strike you? _____

    _____

11. Do you agree with the author that you already have some of every characteristic necessary for success? Yes ☐ No ☐ Why?_____

    _____

SEE YOU AT THE TOP

from the "*I CAN" Course: Intermediate Level Student Manual*, The Zig Ziglar Corporation.

CREATIVE ENCOUNTER #4.........Find-the-Word Puzzle

```
V Y H O U P L X E U C K E P H Y T I L I B A J
U J A I T Q H P P G B P H J J G N Z Q W Y C P
P J P M Z S Q G M T Q P T H H K K K K J K W K
G W P W K Q G R W P P F B G T H I A W E B Z D
K Q I V E K G R R D W L H I N J — V G R C P F
G W N M D I N J E X Z M P M I V C T N L C B L
N P E O R X F A L A J G R F K Y A G S I D P N
O V S D T A J J E D T Q R F G T N R Y K J E H
P I S E T R V P I O C R L S G A J V P T Z U Y
B F R E E — E N T E R P R I S E L W W I T D L
M K O R I V M D Z R F O U Y V O K F T E R J F
H O A F J U Y E O A L Q P D I H K I A A G L G
B P K — Z S D Q Y W I W F C G F C G F C T U U
Y C Q F M A C I R E M A B B V K N J G L H I M
O J K O Y V F J E I G H T L A E W I C L P M Q
A G X — U C X U L D S R U R F L Y S O A Y Z E
E H K R X V H H Q O D J V B F Y T M D K J D K
P V B I Y Y K N C V W Q Q W A R X Q X K Z B L
S F O A M J Y C F S O P W I O U Q O O M S M F
H R M L I Q E S Z E Z H C N N G S I L Q Y F H
D V R S Y Z Q O D A W V G A G Q F D I H N R U
F S S N R T B Q K V T K B I N R O F G H U G Q
L I U H F F U G G Y G L I L Y Z T M E I Z V F
```

FREE-ENTERPRISE
AMERICA
LOVE
HAPPINESS
STRONG
WEALTH
GREAT
CITIZEN
ABILITY
AIR-OF-FREEDOM
I-CAN
THE
FLAG

Directions:

Find the words at the left in the puzzle and circle them carefully. The letters of the words may be arranged horizontally, vertically, or diagonally in either direction.

SEE YOU AT THE TOP

INDEPENDENT PROJECTS—ZIGLAR

1. To build your self-image, make a list of your positive qualities on a card and keep it for handy reference. List your key resources, identify their major strengths, and indicate how they are going to help you attain your goals.
2. In your public library locate copies of and read *The Memory Book* and *Remembering People: The Key to Success*. Learn techniques to train your memory.
3. Choose topics and make up your own crossword puzzles or find-the-word puzzles.
4. Write letters to your congressmen and senators. State your opinions about the problems in America.
5. Study the issues dealing with local government problems. Conduct a city council meeting in your classroom. Role play chief officials.
6. Choose a news article, cartoon, or editorial. Discuss and reproduce how you think that item might appear in a newspaper of a country under a dictatorship.
7. Define free enterprise. List the advantages that the free enterprise system has over communism. What can you do to strengthen America and the free enterprise system?
8. Read about our American heritage. Search for unusual facts about Americans who have influenced our nation's history. Write about their childhood, talents, interests, attitudes, goals and accomplishments.
9. Research American historical places, such as Independence hall, Monticello, and the Capitol Building. Include illustrations with your report.

RESOURCE BOOKS—ZIGLAR

Andrist, Ralph K., ed. *The American Heritage: History of the Making of the Nation*. New York: American Heritage Publishing Co., Inc., 1968.

Commager, Henry Steele. *The Great Constitution: A Book for Young Americans*. New York: The Bobbs-Merrill Co., Inc., 1961.

Folsom, Franklin. *Give Me Liberty: America's Colonial Heritage*. New York: Rand McNally & Co., 1974.

Kane, Joseph Nathan. *Facts About the Presidents*. New York: The H. W. Wilson Co., 1981.

Kane, Joseph Nathan. *Famous First Facts*. 4th ed., expanded and rev. New York: The H. W. Wilson Co., 1981.

Landmarks of Liberty. Maplewood, New Jersey: Hammond, Inc., 1970.

Lorayne, Harry, and Jerry Lucas. *The Memory Book*. New York: Ballantine Books, 1974.

Lorayne, Harry. *Remembering People: The Key to Success*. New York: Warner Books, Inc., 1975.

McCullough, Mamie. *The "I CAN" Course: Intermediate Level Student Manual*. Dallas: The Zig Ziglar Corporation, 1981.

Miers, Earl Schenck. *America and Its Presidents* New York: Grosset & Dunlap, Inc., 1982.

Miers, Earl Schenck. *The Bill of Rights*. New York: Grosset & Dunlap, Inc., 1968.

Seuling, Barbara. *The Last Cow on the White House Lawn & Other Little-Known Facts About the Presidency*. Garden City, New York: Doubleday & Co., Inc., 1978.

Ziglar, Zig. *See You at the Top*. Gretna, Louisiana: Pelican Publishing Co., Inc., 1977.